SELF-ISH

SELF-ISH

a transgender awakening

CHLOE SCHWENKE

 Red Hen Press | *Pasadena, CA*

Book design by Hannah Moye

Library of Congress Cataloging-in-Publication Data

Names: Schwenke, Chloe, author.
Title: Self-ish: a transgender awakening / by Chloe Schwenke.
Description: Pasadena, CA: Red Hen Press, [2018]
Identifiers: LCCN 2017054802 | ISBN 9781597096089 | eISBN 9781597096966
Subjects: LCSH: Schwenke, Chloe. | Transgender people—United
    States—Biography. | Transgender people—Identity.
Classification: LCC HQ77.8.S39 A3 2018 | DDC 306.76/80973—dc23
LC record available at https://lccn.loc.gov/2017054802

The National Endowment for the Arts, the Los Angeles County Arts Commission, the Ahmanson Foundation, the Dwight Stuart Youth Fund, the Max Factor Family Foundation, the Pasadena Tournament of Roses Foundation, the Pasadena Arts & Culture Commission and the City of Pasadena Cultural Affairs Division, the City of Los Angeles Department of Cultural Affairs, the Audrey & Sydney Irmas Charitable Foundation, the Kinder Morgan Foundation, the Allergan Foundation, the Riordan Foundation, and the Amazon Literary Partnership partially support Red Hen Press.

First Edition
Red Hen Press
www.redhen.org

ACKNOWLEDGMENTS

This book would never have been written had it not been for the many family and friends who helped me become who I am today. Some of these people saved my life. There's no one more remarkable and filled with grace, understanding, and caring in my life than my former wife and still dear friend, Christine Lucas, who is the mother of our two children, Ian and Audrey. I also take this opportunity to express my gratitude for Christine's father and my former father-in-law, Robert (Bob) Lucas, who never took the easy path of blaming me, and whose affection for me has been a constant.

I also now recognize the loving support and wisdom of my only sister, Barb Cartmell, who helped ground and support me in some of the most challenging moments of my gender transition, and who helped me through the early drafts of this book. Other family members also did their part, especially my sister-in-law Carol Schwenke. Others who are due a special mention include my cousins Sue Gould, Judy Brill, Dottie Fay, and Stephanie Gould Peteves and their respective husbands Ron Cherry, Larry Brill, Jack Fay, Stathis Peteves, my cousin Prissy Gould, and my niece Tracy Lynn Wolf Dickey and her husband Craig. Some family members initially struggled to greater and lesser degrees with the impact of my gender transition, but never turned their back on the love and loyalty that defined our relationship. These include my three brothers Roger, George, and Ken Schwenke, and their respective wives Carol, Janet, and Amanda Schwenke.

Other remarkable and accepting friends made an enormous difference in my emergence as Chloe. I am thinking particularly of the very wise and caring Susan Collin Marks, the warmly energetic and fiercely loyal Julie Haines, and friends whose immediate acceptance of me was unreserved and unflinching: Lori Keleher Bursum, Jody DeVoll, Tony Dowling and his late wife Karen Vondy, Bobby Herman and Barbara Wein, Joanna and Bill Good, Carrie Hessler-Radelet, Ajit Joshi, Kaisi Kalambo, Sarah Kihika, Veronika Martin, Ryan McCannell, the late Peter Nicholson, Byaruhanga Rukooko, Dan Smit and his two daughters Alexia and Olivia, Victoria Stanski, and Peter and Ann Straub.

Members of my Quaker community were also central to my efforts to transition without undue havoc to my family and my community, and to grounding my transition in spiritual truths. These include my dear British Quaker friends Diana Galvin and the late Patrick Perkins, and too many American Quaker friends to list them all. Still, I will call special attention to: Joanna Axtmann, Alexander Barnes, Carol Beigel and Martha Gay, Phil Callahan, Robalee Chapin, Ann Clendenin, June Confer, Justin Conner, Windy Cooler, Jen Cort, Charlotte and Tim Croft, Karen Cunnyngham, Peter Curtis, Janice Fain Dean, Sara Dean, Lainie and Rob Duncan, Alison Duncan, Ann Dunne, Jade Eaton, Randall Ehrbar and Shawn MacDonald, Mary Ellsberg and Michael Levi, Amy Greene, Anna Goodman, Jamesen Goodman, Shelley Grow, Mosi Harrington and Molly Parrish, Jane Heil, Mary Ann Heller-Hopkins, Carole Hoage, Tom Horne, Paul Jolly, Somers Knight, Ray Lane, Matty Lau, Kit Mason, Samantha McGrath, Catherine McHugh, John Meyer, Cheryl Morden and Ruben Snipper, Anne Marie Moriarty, Joy and Michael Newheart, Karen O'Brien, Sandy Overby, Philip Payette, Leanne Poteet, Kate Prager, Richard Renner and Laura Yeomans, Jolee Robinson, Susannah Hills Rose, Kathy Selvaggio, Marcy Seitel, Joan Spinner, Jacob Stone, Annie Storr, Sharon Stout, Traci and Walter Sullivan, Peterson Toscano, Martha and Steve Woods, Toby Woods, Angela Toda, Margaret Weigers Vitullo, Judy Anne Williams, Tom Wolfe, Anne Wright-Lohaus, Robb Yurisko, and the late Deborah James.

Other friends remained constant in their deep support and affection for me, before, during, and after my transition. Among this group I would include my dear friends: Paul Canning, Peter and Maggie Grayson, Bharat Gupta, Stacy Kosko, Corbin Lyday, Randal Mason, Sisanda Mbokotho, Ada Piazze, Debbie Wicker, Sheila and Mike Wood, and Zakithi Zama.

There are also people in my career who stood by me as my name and persona changed, or as they worked with me as Chloe. These include my most important academic mentor David Crocker and his wife Eddie, Mariclaire Acosta, Indira Ahuwalia, Anna Amato, Keith Berner, Brian Bond, Annie Boyajian, Wendy Bradford, Aimee Breslow, Jesse Bunch, Paul Cadario, Chas Cadwell, Marianne Camerer, Michael Curtis, Sylvia Ellison, Matthew Emry, Leslie Evertz, Anna Franklin, Chris Fry, Bob Gilchrist, Nicole Graham, Melanie Greenberg, Christina Hartman, Sirkku Hellsten, Josh Kaufman, Katherine Raphaelson, the late Andy E. Rice, Steve Roth, Carol Sahley, Mona Siam, Barbara Smith, Joe and Caroline Stepanik, Aili Tripp, and Cameron Wolf.

I also express my gratitude to some of my closest lesbian, gay, bisexual, transgender, queer, and intersex (LGBTQI) sisters and brothers, as well as some deeply committed LGBTQI allies, including: Selim Aratürk, Nisha Ayub, Ambassador Daniel Baer, Lara Ballard, Emmi Bee, Jesse Bernstein, Jim Best, Dana Beyer, Hua Boonyapisomparn, Mike Bosia, Mark Bromley, Clare Byarugaba, Ann Clendenin, Ty Cobb, Phil Crehan, Masen Davis, Petra Doan, Julie Dorf, Andres Rivera Duarte, Justus Eisfeld, Dawn Ennis, Colleen Fay, Laura Garcia, Jamie-Lynn Garvin, Ambassador Michael Guest, Daniel Hinkle, Céleste Twistor Hogan, Fabrice Houdart, Audrey Mbugua Ithibu, Julius Kaggwa, Marko Karadzic, Beyoncé Karungi, JoAnne Keatley, Mara Keisling, Kath Khangpiboon, Kent Klindera, Amélie Erin Koran, Oleg Kucheryavenko, Joy Ladin, Ian Lekus, Steve Letsike, Samir Luthur, Barbra Maruga, Nikilas Mawanda, Sarah McBride, Helen McConnell, Robyn McCutcheon, Jessica McKinnon, Deyone Milana, Victor Mukasa, Michael Namalum, Ochieng Ochieng, Pepe-Julian Onziema, Dylan Orr, Randy Orso, Chris Paige, Prempreeda Pramoj, Jabu Pereira, Laura Perry, Xulaye Cleo Quentaro, Mia Quetzal, Allyson Robinson, Michelle Ross, Susan Rowe, Diego Sanchex, Eric Scharf, Davida Schiffer, Ed Settle, Simran Shaikh, Amanda Simpson, Sheri Swokowski, Brynn Tannehill, Jetsada Taesombat, Diane Ullius, Caroline Vagneron, Kim Vance, Angel Ventura, and Jeffrey Waite.

Finally, I take special pleasure in recognizing the long-standing friendship of my wise, worldly, and exceptionally competent electrologist Mona Wexler, my amazing voice therapist Tish Moody, and my remarkably gifted therapist Martha Harris.

To Christine, Ian, and Audrey

CONTENTS

FAITH, ETHICS, AND LEADINGS

OWNING A PAST, RESTARTING A LIFE

TRANSGENDER LIFE, CHLOE LIFE

SELF-ISH

PROLOGUE

"You'll be snapped up in no time. They'll be so lucky to have you!"
I heard variations on this theme from a number of well-wishers after I unexpectedly lost my job at a leading human rights organization in November of 2014. I have little doubt that my status as a transgender feminist was a significant—and perhaps decisive—factor in this termination. As a trans woman of a certain age, I was nearly immobilized with worry as I contemplated the anticipated difficulties inherent in finding a new job. Still, I'm very good at what I do, and I do have a wealth of experience. I'm a leader, I'm smart, and I care about people. I'm good at mentoring, motivating, and meeting expectations, and I'm pragmatic and strategic in my executive duties. I get great results through teamwork and collaboration, while being sensitive to time and money. I'm outstanding at public speaking. Most importantly, I have a great deal of emotional intelligence, I'm articulate, and I'm passionate about the work that I do in human rights activism and international development.

How many women would write those words about themselves?

An assertive white male upbringing has its benefits. As a child and young adult I was exhorted time and time again to push myself, and to speak out when opportunities arose. Residual modesty aside, I actually do believe it's a reasonably accurate self-assessment. Of course I've made some dreadful mistakes, and I haven't always exercised the best judgment. I've had my bad days. Still, as executive-level staff go in my industry, I'm pretty damn good. As for executive staff who also happen to be transgender, I'm terrific, given the scarcity of transgender persons in that role. If only prospective employers could find their way to the same conclusion.

The Christmas holidays came and went, three times. They've now just passed, and I'm in that fairly dire time of year when I wonder if I can really make it through the frigid, bleak winter months ahead. What's there to look forward to? Spring seems far too remote, and I'm not exactly high on anyone's Valentine's Day list. And as I ponder the winter doldrums, I'm aware that no one is yet snapping, even if there are a few possibilities. I regularly apply for jobs that I'm exceptionally well qualified for, but I don't often get invited to interviews. I don't make any declarations in my resume or cover letter that I have a gender nonconforming past, yet that truth is but a Google-click away. Yes, I've worked my network thoroughly, and it's a very good network, but the offers as yet are not forthcoming and the requests for employment interviews are scarce. Even consulting work can prove spotty to find.

This situation isn't without precedent in my life. When I first transitioned gender, my employer at the time felt embarrassed to have clients meet with me and in short order I was terminated from that job. A similarly earnest effort of job hunting ensued, but in those days I was only looking for a technical job or a post at middle management. I found some consulting work, mostly writing proposals, but no full-time jobs were accessible. Nothing changed until one day the phone rang and the State Department asked me to come in to interview for a job I'd never applied for, as a senior political appointee of the Obama administration. Miracles do happen; some governments do appear to be less squeamish at the prospect of hiring a transgender person in a prominent, very public role. Thank goodness. But that was then; now we are entering a very dark political time for anyone who is transgender. I have no delusions as to the manner in which the Trump administration will respond to the needs and aspirations of lesbian, gay, bisexual, transgender, queer, or intersex (LGBTQI) American citizens.

When that unexpected phone call came back in 2010, the world was far different. Barack Obama was in the White House, and being transgender wasn't seen as a freakish liability or a moral failing. After a lengthy but usual ordeal of interviews and security clearances, I embarked upon what was to become almost three years of being secure in my government job. Then, for reasons I have yet to entirely unravel, it struck me that it was time to change jobs. Perhaps I was operating under the old adage that "it's always best to find your next job while you still have your current job." As a political appointee, my job as Senior Advisor on Democracy, Human Rights, and Governance for Africa at the US Agency for International Development would have been fairly secure for another four years, as President Obama had just won re-election. I could have easily hunkered down and stayed put, and in hindsight I probably should have. Instead, I reasoned that as a political appointee my primary duty was to be an agent of change. I was there to prod and poke and help to move a large government bureaucracy along a path that aligned more closely with the vision articulated by my boss, President Obama. I'd thrown myself into that, and had been effective in helping to shape significant policy changes that achieved the beginnings of that realignment. As time went by, however, being an *embedded* change agent achieved diminishing results as change-resistant bureaucrats learned workarounds. "Yes, dear" became a polite proxy for "I'm not going to do that." I had begun to feel like my service in the government was no longer effectual.

Then there was the other reason. My appointment as the first transgender political appointee in the federal foreign affairs agencies, and one of only four openly transgender appointees ever (at that time) throughout the whole of the vast federal government, was momentous. It felt to me like a glass ceiling had been broken; many transgender friends from around the world had written to me to say how much this appointment meant for them, as well as how happy they were for me. Getting that appointment was the news, not staying in that role for an extended period of time. My career goal was and always has been to generate beneficial impact through my work. When people in my network advised me that the position of vice president for global programs at the nation's oldest human rights organization was being advertised, I threw my hat into the ring.

Very promptly the letter from the president of that organization came back. Thanks, but no thanks. It was an unexpected response; several well-placed persons within that institution had assured me that I would be a strong candidate for the job. The president of that organization at that time however had determined otherwise, sight of me unseen. Only through the strenuous intervention of some people on his executive staff was he convinced that he might be doing the organization a disservice not to at least give me the benefit of an interview. The rejection letter was awkwardly retracted, an interview scheduled, and the interview went well. Soon I was hired. And yes, I did a great job, by any rational measure. Still, on his next to last day as president, he fired me. No one on their board of directors intervened, even though they knew me and were very familiar with my considerable accomplishments. With the president's announced departure, they'd even interviewed me as his possible replacement. Although a finalist, I did not get that job, and while the person who was hired for that role had wonderful qualifications, a part of me is left wondering whether that prominent human rights organization wasn't quite ready to have a trans woman (and feminist) as their primary point of contact with the world. Or even whether they were ready to have me at all; as a trans woman executive I knew that I thought differently than my white and cisgender (i.e., non-transgender) male colleagues. While I viewed that different perspective as an asset and a true benefit of diversity, it would appear that the outgoing president thought otherwise. In this world, dominant male power almost always prevails, even on its way out the door.

As the weeks and months of unemployment have ticked by since that late 2014 termination, there may be larger questions here. First, are Americans ready for an openly (if not in-your-face) transgender woman with a PhD and more than three decades of experience to compete for and hold an executive job? Any senior job? Second, should I have just forgotten about the traditional job market and the more pedestrian concerns of a reliable paycheck to instead dedicate my remaining years of work to focus on advocacy about the issue nearest to my heart—recognizing the human dignity of transgender persons globally? Or third, did I have even the faintest idea at that time how challenging the world can be for a trans woman of sixty-plus years to find a job at all? If I had known the mountain ahead of me, would I have sought some path around it instead of beginning that exhausting climb?

The third question is the most straightforward. Looking backward is easy; looking forward from where I sit now is nothing short of daunting. If nothing else since losing that job late in 2014, I now know firsthand and without question that being an older trans woman in this world is exceptionally hard. While I had some doubts in November 2014, I really had no idea how steep and hard the path ahead would be, and how little it had to do with me being me. I was being flung out—jobless and with very modest savings—to begin a climb that would teach me how much the world views people as abstractions, as "an old person" and as "transgender." No one had the time or inclination to get beyond those labels to the person behind them: me.

Which takes me directly back to that first question that I posed above: Is America ready for us? In American culture the prevailing stereotypes of transgender women may be less malicious and brutal than their equivalents in some other cultures, but they're certainly not flattering. Quite the opposite. Comedians find gender-nonconforming stereotypes great for a laugh, but for those of us on the other end of their humor these misrepresentations of transgender persons are awful, even pernicious, always insensitive, and decidedly hurtful. Most American attitudes about transgender people have been and continue to be formed and sustained by such stereotypes, and are exacerbated by profound ignorance, a perverse and callous sense of humor, a fear of "the other," and—as seen in the recent election—by right-wing political ideologies that make a virtue out of rejecting diversity. Just thinking about people like me makes many Americans squeamish; particularly many American men. Yet more troublesome still is that many—most—Americans really have never thought about us at all, at least until the media frenzy surrounding the splashy coming-out of Caitlyn Jenner. But Ms. Jenner aside, Americans have had very little reason to reflect on the plight of transgender folk; we're few in number and hence their chances of having had any significant interaction with us—like hiring one of us—are statistically unlikely.

Thankfully, there have been exceptions. Under President Obama most of the federal government made outstanding and rapid progress in avoiding or overcoming prejudice against transgender job applicants, and evaluating the merits of such candidates objectively. Even the military edged closer to acceptance of transgender service members, and the formal ban against transgender servicemen and women has recently been lifted. Whether that ban returns under Trump has yet to be seen.

Obama's policy for the rest of the federal government, as stated by the Office of Personnel Management, was to treat all employees with dignity and respect and to prohibit discrimination in the workplace based on any employee's ethnicity or race, national origin, gender, religion, sexual orientation, political affiliation, disability, marital status, and sex—the latter was interpreted to include transgender persons.

That was then; we are now in a world turned upside down, with a president who has selected senior staff who look on the likes of me with genuine disdain, abhorrence, or worse. I'm now led to push back fiercely on this turnaround, and while my voice isn't a loud one, I still proudly identify as one of Hillary Clinton's "nasty women."

Outside of government, transgender persons in America appear to be finding more job opportunities at entry-level and even mid-level positions, although the data so far is mostly anecdotal. What data does exist (such as the recently published 2015 US Transgender Survey, by the National Center for Transgender Equality), however, is hardly heartening. At least there's a rapidly growing list of online and institutional resources to guide transgender job seekers through various state laws and nondiscrimination provisions, but job applicants won't be told that the reason they are not offered the job is because they are trans. Trying to pursue legal remedies against employment discrimination is always more theoretical than realistic; employers know better than to open themselves up to such actions. They just say "no." Some colleges, universities, faith-based groups, and even some private firms resolutely claim the right to discriminate against gay and transgender persons (on freedom of religion grounds). Let's see how that all plays out under Trump.

My best hope for my transgender brothers and sisters lies with the young. In my view, the rapid increase of awareness and commitment to diversity by many better-educated, younger Americans does offer significant promise for the future. For now, however, top-level jobs in the private sector are not particularly accessible to transgender applicants. My own fraught experience has taught me that it's hard even to get past the stereotypes to secure an invitation to a job interview. Of course, given the stigmatized and often troubled individual histories of most transgender persons who struggle to get by in a society that is very disinclined to embrace them, even achieving an appropriate stage of education and accomplishment to become competitive for good jobs is a rarity.

My own job struggle has convinced me that—fair or not—the door to a senior career position is almost entirely shut for people like me, unless someone on the inside is keeping it open just a crack. Once through that door, it's up to us—to me—to make my case. Other marginalized Americans have walked this path before me: women, persons of color, religious and ethnic minorities, persons with disabilities. Many job applicants never get invited to the interview not because of their qualifications, but because of who they are. They've made significant progress but have yet to find that level playing field and may never entirely overcome their marginalization. But it all requires such stamina, resilience, and ultimately such self-confidence. I will need to return and reread my self-flattering opening paragraphs of this book again and again just to stay in the fight. Go girl!

It's clear to me, as I learn more and more about the lives of people like me in America, that transgender women are only beginning this journey. It's always a steep trek up a formidable mountain. Sometimes we find jobs as hairdressers, admin assistants, or waitresses. A few of us find professional careers, or manage to reclaim professional status after a gender transition. A very small number are entrepreneurs, who have the knowledge, cunning, and resources to set up their own successful companies or non-profit organizations. Many transgender men also face similar challenges, but the existence of transgender men is less of a scandal to

American society, and transgender men are far more successful at "going stealth"—blending in to mainstream society—and just getting on with their lives. That is, unless new bathroom bills appear, and transgender men are forced to start using women's public restrooms.

I haven't forgotten my second question. Advocacy is the life that calls to me each day, as I reflect on the many personal experiences that this book describes, and on the dire plight of transgender persons globally. I once took the position that our beleaguered if resilient struggle for societal recognition of our fundamental humanity was both compelling and wrenching—that it inspired within me a deep passion to advocate on their behalf. Now I know better—I am not an insulated observer of "transgender persons globally." If nothing else, the grueling months since November 2014 have opened my eyes to the reality that I am one of them. I am one of "those people." I am they, and it is truly hard.

Being of them and with them in this struggle doesn't pay my bills or give me any comfort about my encroaching journey into old age, but it does energize me. While I take no personal credit for it, I recognize that I have within me an advocacy voice that has the power to reach people and may even lead to some tangible changes for the better. I damn well better put that voice to some good use while I still can, and give it my best shot, even if it awakens the army of transphobic Internet trolls who relish finding targets like me. They've already started doing just that, and I had to go through the rough process of learning that it never helps to respond to any of their messages. These are hard times for trans folk, but we're not going away.

Still, indignant me notwithstanding, I know that this type of advocacy is a path without any evident adequate means of financial support. No global or regional institutions outside of just a handful (such as the National Center for Transgender Equality) have identified or funded such a platform, and their financial resources are—well—thin. There's just no getting around it. The plight of transgender persons globally is dire and we are few, hence our issues are viewed as relatively inconsequential (or at least a low-priority) to most human rights, research, and development organizations.

Where does that leave me? Hopefully this book will begin to answer that question by filling in the picture of who that "me" is. My humanity, my story, is my gift. How I seize that gift remains my future journey's objective, and its opportunity.

Even human rights advocates have to pay for rent, health care, and groceries. Maybe some cosmetics, a new dress, an occasional Guinness . . . and then I have never yet been on a cruise, or flown business class. It's not all selfless sacrifice for the greater good. I know that the path of direct advocacy is unrealistic and unsustainable without self-care, and without a great deal of moral, economic, and logistical support. Without a steady income and some savings, it is a fool's errand. Very little of that infrastructure is accessible or even exists for those of us who advocate for transgender issues globally, and while arguably there is great virtue and honor in tilting at windmills, even Don Quixote de la Mancha had funding. My advocacy may therefore have to be less direct and less of a full-time commitment. Who knows? Hopefully by the time I finish writing this book I'll know. Perhaps I will have found that elusive next job, or will have found a way to generate sufficient consulting work to sustain myself. I have no intention of curling up and dying. As you'll see when you read my story, that's not what this girl is about.

My struggle to participate in American life while still holding myself in genuine solidarity with those in deepest need around the world—economically, socially, democratically, spiritually—is hardly unique among transgender women. And while that struggle is shared, my own story is unique and very human.

This book is intended to share just that one story, my story. Behind that story is simply one woman, a very self-ish woman.

SELF-ISHNESS AND AUTHENTICITY

Photograph by Ian Schwenke

A QUESTION OF SANITY, A JOURNEY OF CHOICE

The CEO was already thirty minutes late for the lunch appointment that a mutual friend had facilitated. Gathering what was left of my pride, I headed out the door, only to run into him a short distance up the street heading in my direction. He was profusely apologetic, and given how desperate I was for some help in my job hunt, I was ready to forgive. Neither of us were hungry by that stage, so we grabbed our mugs of chai and headed up the stairs to the small dining area. Together we engaged in the intricate verbal dance of getting acquainted, finding out which countries, people, and life-shaping experiences we had in common. The conversation flowed easily, at least until I made some reference to the challenges of overcoming my *history* as I looked for that next executive job.

"What history?"

"I'm a transgender woman." I was surprised that in the small world of Washington international development practitioners that he didn't already know, or perhaps I was flattering myself that he might have Googled me before this get-together and come to the lunch with that knowledge. He hadn't, but there was no going back. The entire conversation changed, not in a bad way, but certainly not along any pathway that would lead us back to how he might be able to assist me in that elusive and increasingly urgent quest: to find a job before I became penniless. He asked the usual questions that most men ask when they find out my past, while anxiously trying to avoid the awkward parts. He asked if I was happy in my new life, and if my family had been supportive. He asked if the transition had been well received (although by whom was not part of his question). And he verged into the more sensitive topics when he asked if it had been difficult to learn to live as a woman. Fortunately, he did not ask about any surgeries I might have had, what my sexual orientation had been and now was, or whether I was now both legally and biologically female—I (and probably most transgender persons) would have found these latter questions to be inappropriate. So he scored well by not asking them; I waited for his next conversational direction. He said nothing.

I too stopped talking. He just smiled, intently and with a fixed stare that held a meaning I couldn't quite fathom. We held the silence for a prolonged period—easy for me since, as a Quaker, silence is my natural element. Finally, he spoke again, wrapping up the conversation by stating that his organization was very unlikely to have any work for me. There wasn't anything mean or unpleasant about this declaration, but there was nothing unclear about it either. As we parted outside the restaurant, on that first spring-like day of last year, his long and quiet stare continued to haunt me. There was something searching, bemused, and inquiring about it. What did he think of me, really?

We all start by questioning our sanity.

Demonstrated and consistent rationality over time is the key to anyone's claim of sanity; yet is it rational that people like me make everything so complicated? Using the sex-derived binary that we've come to know as gender, societies have gone to considerable lengths to enshrine and protect gender-specific privileges, roles, and obligations—in short, how power, wealth, opportunities, and often even dignity are allocated. This goes deep; it's very hard to imagine that there is any stronger anthropological or sociological classification of greater durability and inviolability across the millennia than that between men and women.

What sane individual would attempt to rock that boat?

While there are some (and perhaps many) who would disagree, it is my own conviction that no one would *want* to be transgender. After all, the gender binary does have some soft edges, even if the sex binary appears to be more rigidly assigned. History puts forth occasional examples of persons who through their behavior or convictions stood on the very farthest margins of their assigned gender classification, yet seldom are such figures respected or treated as anything but curiosities, or worse. Those on the fringe hardly mattered until relatively recently, when the previously absurd prospect of a person actually making the physiological leap to inhabit a differently sexed body and gender identity became plausible. These new gray spaces that have recently opened up between the strict male-female gender and sex categories leave many people confused, perplexed, even irate. Who asked for this? Some people are beginning to question whether body itself defines gender or sex. Are gender-confirming surgeries even necessary for transgender people to be who they claim to be? It's a revolutionary notion, and not one warmly embraced by the majority of cisgender folk who are finding life already becoming unpleasantly complex. A woman with a penis? Yes. Why not?

Medical and surgical science notwithstanding, who was I to think I could wipe away all those decades of my life in which I had been comprehensively socialized into that originally assigned male sex and the associated gender identity? Who was I to think I could relocate myself from one body-sex to another, regardless of my original label? Who was I to intentionally straddle the boundary between the audacious and the absurd? Transgender metaphors never quite capture the realities we endure, but the image of leaping from the roof of one outrageously tall building to another is apt, in the sense that the person contemplating the leap is poignantly aware of the consequences of not quite going the full distance. There's the added dimension that even if you make it to that other rooftop you really don't know if a welcome awaits you inside that building; it may look like a building that shines brightly, but you've never been on the inside. Then there's the lingering worry that those on the inside may push you out of the nearest window.

You are also aware that the option of jumping back to where you started is not available, no matter how majestically you might make that original leap. For me and many like me, this isn't about gender tourism; it's a one-way journey in which everything is at stake. Nearly all cisgender folk fail to realize that the metaphorical tall building of gender identity that we leapt from was itself engulfed in the consuming flames of what we call dissonance. Our only choice was to jump.

Perhaps I'm making too much of the gender binary metaphor, the either-or. For some intrepid transgender folk, there's the option of unilaterally shifting the terms of engagement through the wholesale rejection of the gender and sex binary. The choice to be self-defined outside the almost universal male or female categories of imposed gender roles and identity is a bold one, given nearly everyone else's unrelenting pressure for you to plant your flag on one "side" or the other. If you really must transgress the binary, most would say, it would be far better to just be discreet or secretive about it so that cisgender folk needn't be inconvenienced by those remarkably strong individuals who claim that category of "genderqueer"—that place between gender roles and expectations. I salute my genderqueer and androgynous colleagues, and I will continue to advocate that their identity be respected as legitimate and viable.

I will also continue to argue that society needs to accommodate the gender continuum so that we all can have a crack at being genuinely human and genuinely ourselves at any point along that continuum. For me, however, that in-between option held no appeal; I was born to be a woman—it just took a while. I had the relative luxury of clarity of mind and spirit to accept that for me the binary could work, if only I could relocate myself from one pole to the other, which in turn meant that perhaps I had indeed taken leave of my senses. I won't pretend that this possibility never entered my mind; it would be more realistic to acknowledge that I frequently wrestled with the absurdity of "me against the whole world." How could everyone else—especially people who loved me and whose wisdom I relied upon—be so wrong about who I am? It is a question probably every transgender person confronts, and it leads directly to other questions. Am I simply delusional, or am I so self-centered that I'm unable to acknowledge the gender classification that was so clearly manifested in my private parts and socialized into me by those who knew best?

Rising above the debilitating questions (many of them self-inflicted) about one's own authentic sense of identity is not a given. We fight for that. Those who know best enjoy their authority, and they fiercely resist those such as I who venture to say: "Wait a minute—that's not me." As I and probably all transgender persons come to learn, even the monumental feat of overcoming the authoritative and rejecting strictures of "those who know best" does nothing to undo or rewrite one's personal history. While now I happily occupy a woman's body and am widely accepted by society as such, I remain a woman who never had a girlhood. I watch as my own daughter grows up and experiences the emotional roller coaster of high school, navigating all the intricate interrelationships, feuds, cliques, intrigues, and social boundaries. I marvel at the tight friendships she develops in which one's vulnerability is owned (and not denied, as boys are socialized to do). I know with some vicarious certainty that American girls such as my daughter are shaped and changed by participating in their world of girl space, from learning the latest news of interest, deliberating who is hot on YouTube, sharing tips on makeup and fashion, or thinking about politics—and talking about boys. And I even see it continue across generations, as daughters frequently push back strongly against their biological mothers, only to cling tightly to them moments later in a form of conspiratorial communication that I'm not party to.

Many women tell me how lucky I am to have avoided that awkward and turbulent stage of life, but I'm not so sure. I feel its absence, frequently, even if that void eludes any explicit description. What I am sure of is that the teenage-girl stage of adolescence—and all that flows from those sets of experiences and relationships—is no longer accessible to adults who transition gender from male to female embodiment later in life.

Having missed the unique chrysalis of girlhood, in the eyes of others my integrity as a woman can thereby become suspect. You needn't spend very much time among feminists to stumble upon those second-wave folks who militantly align with the "womyn-born womyn" movement, explicitly rejecting my claim of gender authenticity. To them, I can never be a woman (or "womyn") because I wasn't embodied as one at birth, and I wasn't raised as Chloe. Transgender women are not authentic, and I learned quickly to avoid asking them what they then think I am. Fortunately for me, such gender-policing women are few in number and at the fringes—albeit loudly so. I've experienced nothing but a consistent warm embrace and welcome from most women I have met, after they learn that I am transgender. Warm embraces are in exceptionally short supply however from any of the men whom I've (briefly) dated, once they are enlightened regarding my curious gender history. I've yet to meet a plausible romantic male prospect who can avoid the knee-jerk reaction of either abhorrence or self-righteous indignation once they learn about my status as woman-without-girlhood. Watching men behave badly as they go through the "freaked out" and "outraged" male display is painful and wrenching. Acting out of emotional self-preservation, I've put my dating aspirations on indefinite hold.

The authenticity questions linger on. If we are not fully-fledged women, who and what are we? We are transgender women, or "trans women." I am growing to accept that label and its inescapability, seeing it not so much as a less-than-genuine description and instead a calling-out of our rarity and distinction. Still, it remains a thrill for me simply to be "she," to be a woman out and about in the world, which is who I am in the vast majority of my daily interactions.

Woman or trans woman, those of us who manage to claim ourselves and find that place of peace within often have a curious adjective applied to us: audacious. Some of us also get called pretty, or femme, or even mysterious, but being seen as audacious is far more validating to a transgender person in its commendable traits of assertiveness, determination, and courage. Being so flattered is tempered only by the realization that any gender transition exemplified by such honorable traits still comes at a very high cost to all others who have deep investments in our originally assigned gender. It's awkward enough for coworkers, bosses, siblings, friends, and social acquaintances to reclassify their views of your identity and get those troublesome pronouns where they should be. Many will balk and push back—sometimes fiercely. Yet when it comes to negotiating this transition with parents, a spouse (or significant other), and offspring, "audacious" often becomes "selfish."

How dare I do this?

Reactions vary enormously when transgender people come out, especially when they express their intention to transition. For me, as described later in this book, coming out wasn't always met with warmth, grace and love as those close to me learned that I was transgender. People informed me, using that unmistakable voice of assuredness and authority, that I was delusional, wrong-headed, immoral, or simply being absurd. The angriest and most common negative reaction was that I was being inexcusably selfish. There were often many additional adjectives added to "selfish," but the sentiment was clear. How can I do "this" to my wife, my children, my extended family, or my friends? By doing "this," I saw my relationship with some siblings and a few close friends disintegrate—in the case of my siblings only gradually to be retrieved over a protracted period. I saw my second marriage end, although the woman who was once my wife remains a very dear and trusted friend. "This" led a Ugandan colleague to struggle to know how to react; his pastor in the Ugandan capital Kampala categorically advised him that I was an abomination in the eyes of the Lord and that he should therefore have nothing more to do with me. That's pretty definitive.

While authenticity is widely valued, selfishness is perhaps an odd attribute to celebrate. There are other less controversial compliments directed at transgender persons; we're often heralded as brave, courageous, honest, or determined. I've chosen, however, to befriend the "selfish" label, probably because it so disarms those who select this way of demeaning me. And given the abundant pernicious and humiliating stereotypes about transgender persons, the list of those whose inherent reaction is to demean me in one way or another is sadly very long. To them "selfish" speaks of being callous, unconcerned and uncaring of the welfare of others. After all, selfish people place their self-interest arrogantly ahead of the legitimate, reasonable needs and feelings of other folk. We aren't limited to accusations of selfishness; there are other similar pejoratives including narcissism, self-absorption, silliness, and being dysfunctional or lacking in sanity.

For transgender people, however, the decision to claim and own one's authentic self is wholesomely *self*-ish. For years (and sometimes decades) we lead lives of painful denial, trying to ignore, dilute, or reject the persistent internal messages and yearnings that finally, inexorably, lead us to where we are now. We've paid the most awful price for not being more self-ish: the hollowness and dissonance of living one's life in the wrong body in adherence to other people's immutable dictates about gender identity and role. The resulting inner tumult is debilitating: bouts of deep depression, troubled relationships with those whom we love, even suicidal ideation. For me, whose teaching, work, and passion is the field of applied ethics, there were periods in which I felt like a complete fraud. Until I confronted my transgender status, I had no way in which to explain or respond to my growing sense of a hollowed-out integrity. It wasn't something I could come to peace with, or at times even bear. I felt undermined in my most deeply held convictions, affections, relationships, and passions—without a "self" that I could love or respect.

It was an awful place to be.

I'm not alone among transgender persons in having adopted, out of necessity, extreme coping methods to deal with my unlovable sense of self—methods that were ultimately very self-destructive. To this day, they are too discomforting to describe and too painful to recall in any detail. All that I can say is that what I did to get by was caustic to my soul and cruel to my then-male body, yet necessary to stay alive. It worked for a while. Not all transgender persons find their own ways to cope. They simply fail; suicide is tragically a too common outcome of this condition.[1]

So I was and am self-ish, but—unlike many who react to me—I was never intentionally callous. In claiming my authenticity, I was and remain aware that in my character and my actions I have an impact on others

---

1. Among the respondents in the National Transgender Discrimination Survey (NTDS), conducted by the National Gay and Lesbian Task Force and National Center for Transgender Equality, the prevalence of suicide attempts is 41 percent. That rate hugely exceeds the 4.6 percent of the overall US population who report a lifetime suicide attempt.

around me. I continue to be amazed and often perplexed at how profound that impact can be for some people, spanning a continuum from delight to abhorrence. Why does being authentic, in this case through my authentic gender expression as a woman, matter so much to those who are not in interdependent relationships with me? Who is it that they wanted—the authentic "me"—or only a person who conformed to whatever particular gender presentation they felt I owed to them?

Before even considering the confusing terrain of gender, "self" is a contentious concept; it has as much to do with psychology, culture, and history as with morality. Are we the product of our societies, shaped by forces over which we have no control? Are we instead the end result of our own creative spirits, a product of the choices we make? Or is there a hidden "true" self within that we must discover through arduous introspection, painfully journeying into those darker regions of the soul? Perhaps all of these alternative explanations offer some degree of truth, in proportions that vary for each of us. From a moral perspective there are important choices to be made: In the face of immense societal pressures to conform to cultural stereotypes and roles that define who "we" are as members of any given community, society, family, relationship and gender, are we left with the morally permissible choice to be our own authentic selves? Are we entitled to be self-ish? And if not, then what?

Transgender people, as we begin the process of coming out, quickly confront the moral precept to "do no harm." This principle is fundamental to the civility, coherence, and vitality of our societies, and forms the metric upon which people's actions—and the consequences that flow from those actions—are judged. We all ought to sacrifice elements of our self-interest so that our families and loved ones will thrive and a larger common good can be achieved, particularly when our sacrifice prevents actual harm to others. Coming out as a transgender person does have potentially harmful consequences for others. Shouldn't we sacrifice our desire to express our authentic gender so that they might thrive?

When husbands cease to be male or wives to be female, when mothers become fathers or vice versa, there's an impact. Innocent people suffer, often deeply, as a consequence of our "choice." Children are deeply affected—their childhood innocence and sweetness should never have been subjected to such a profound threat. My "selfish fixation" was that threat; I was that threat. How could I justify exposing them to this upheaval? What could make this action morally permissible?

Morally permissible? When values conflict, as they often do, we attempt to resolve them within a framework that has boundaries: what is permitted, and what is not. The framework is seldom articulated explicitly, but we have multiple and diverse messages from our society, religion, culture, and community to guide us to where the boundaries are, and to minimize the gray areas. We learn to sense what tradeoffs are "allowed" as we juxtapose one irreconcilable value against another, discerning which value is best placed to guide our actions. Thus did I wrestle with my sense of patriotic obligation when I was placed in a draft-eligible status during the Vietnam War. Thus did my sixteen-year-old daughter Audrey wrestle when I asked if she would accompany me to one of her high school football games—I quickly learned that the hyper-charged and often misogynistic masculinity of many of the boys on that team was anathema to her. School loyalty and even acquiescence to a parental request has its limits; we did not go.

Using this framework of what is permissible, transgender people are urged—directly or by less direct pressure—to constrain our "selfish" tradeoffs. Many pastors and clergy warn us of our sinfully self-indulgent proclivities, and exhort us—for the good of all who know us—to show restraint. What's left unanswered is the extent of our restraint; must we sacrifice our fundamental identity as a human being, so that others' lives will not be disrupted, harmed, or inconvenienced? Should I have come out to my ninety-one-year-old father, or just soldiered through in the boy clothes (at least in his presence) until he passed? That choice—as I relate later—and other decisions that I made as I transitioned all had consequences. It was all a tender negotiation: like everyone, essential aspects of my identity are made manifest in my gender expression. Society demands certainty and consistency in that regard, sometimes (and often grudgingly) with occasional room at the margins for troublesome people like me to discreetly explore our feminine/masculine inclinations. That was the reaction of several people in my own Quaker faith community, who were deeply perplexed that I would pursue so radical a path as a gender transition. One Quaker woman asked a mutual friend: "Can't he find less extreme ways to express his feminine side?" With more than a hint of exasperation, my friend explained that in my situation being female was more than a "side," more indeed than expression or presentation. My Quaker friend's response (even with the correct pronouns): "For Chloe to be herself, gender consciousness isn't on the side. It is at her center." Amen!

Even my friend's insightful answer seemed insufficient to some. After all, their genders were so deeply hardwired into their beings that it wasn't easy for them to disassociate that part of their identities so as to see what was left. The gender lens colors our world view, shapes our moral and emotional experience of our lives and our environments. Testosterone is a powerful drug, and its impact on a person's perceptions and actions should not be ignored or wished away. Almost every aspect of our lives— for better or for worse—is gendered. Transgender persons know very well what's left once gender is stripped away: the very core of human dignity itself. We also know that while there is much to our identities that isn't directly gender-linked, gender remains central and pervasive. So the lingering question stands unanswered: Are we morally permitted to be self-ish when our identity itself is on the line?

Moral permissibility applies not only to our chosen actions and their consequences, but also to our character—who we are. The very quest of pursuing what I fervently believed was my authentic identity appeared to many people as foolhardy and dangerous; I was trading off my decades of investment in the character they knew as Stephen for the sake of some abstract notion of a hidden woman. What would befall the attributes that formed the person known as Stephen, and Stephen's character in a moral sense, when I crossed the gender barrier? Would I become a new person, a blank slate of a character, or would I be bringing something fundamentally "me" and Stephen-esque to this new incarnation? What would I lose when I crossed the gender boundary, besides some great biceps and all those cultural advantages that society assigns to males? Perhaps more importantly, why wasn't I feeling any sense of loss or remorse as I bid masculinity adieu?

When I came out and confided in one Kenyan-American friend, he wistfully spoke of someone he knew who had felt compelled to transition gender. "It did not go well for him," he said flatly. I never even found out if he was talking about a transgender woman (he-to-she) or a transgender man (she-to-he). My friend's comment was all that he had to say on the topic, but it was laden with regret for this unfortunate friend of his. Sharing this observation with me was a message that may not have been intentionally meant for my ears, suffused as it was with genuine sorrow for his friend's plight, but I could not help but wonder (and worry) how he might describe me to others in some future conversation.

It is rare for people to ask me if I have any regrets. It's probably too personal, or too politically incorrect. Still, in the few instances when people have inquired how I feel now (perhaps as they prodded me to disclose some burning regrets), my answer has always been easy and direct. I've never felt better; my only regrets are for any suffering I might have caused to others, and for my many years of having endured the unrelenting pain of life in the wrong body.

Finding the moral boundary between selfish and self-ish isn't easy, and there aren't any hard-and-fast rules about being self-ish. We're all reasonably expected to sacrifice some degree of self-interest for the sake of everyone's flourishing, since civilization and progress ultimately are about flourishing harmoniously as human beings together, in society. Reasonable sacrifices are therefore expected, but I'm convinced that we should never sacrifice our authentic identity, which is the root of our humanity.

A gender transition may well be the only path to authenticity, and for many like me the sole path to staying alive, but it still leaves the question of *when* unanswered. I wrestled with the questions: Would I be causing pain to others by prolonging my life as Stephen, pretending to be someone I am not? What pain would I inflict upon myself by delaying a transition, and was I strong enough to bear it? Was there some virtue in bearing such pain so that others would not be inconvenienced? Given my experience of the corrosive and increasingly debilitating power of gender dissonance, further prolonging my time in the wrong body would have made me a very unpleasant person to be around. More importantly, there was a high probability that I wouldn't have been able to sustain the stress, to "be around" at all if being present as Chloe was to be denied, or indefinitely deferred. There is a limit to how many times someone can look in the mirror and see someone else looking back at them.

I wasn't alone in this dilemma; many transgender parents wrestle mightily about whether they should delay their own transition until after their children are grown, or until elderly parents have passed, even though this almost always entails extreme depression and not infrequently the real risk of suicide by that transgender person. The better question is what quality and richness of authentic relationship between parent and child will be lost, never to be fully retrieved, by being trapped within the wrong identity during their precious years of childhood?

The sanity question persists. As far as I am concerned, no one in their right mind would ever *want* to be transgender. It's a terrible diagnosis to come to terms with; it takes years to adjust to such a new world, and to undertake the transition journey. As transgender persons, we deal with enormous challenges, are subjected to bias and humiliation, labor through prolonged periods of insecurity and awkwardness, struggle to find employment, and often flounder in our attempts to cultivate intimate and caring relationships. Does anyone think for even a minute that if I could've wished this all away, I wouldn't have done so? Yet for better or worse, being transgender is the central fact in my life, and I'm always coming to terms with that. My gender history won't ever go away, nor will my involuntary fixation with viewing the world through a complicated gender lens. It would be comforting to think of myself as some bold and intrepid soul who dared to do the impossible and made it to the other side of the gender transition, in a perilous and uncharted frontier between the sexes. More realistically, and far less heroically, I did what I had to do to stay alive, often feeling powerless to avoid the collateral damage inflicted upon my whole family. I would've loved to have spared everyone (including me) the consequent pain, but I wasn't able. To stay alive, I needed to deal with it. Even when I became fully aware of some of the worst possible outcomes, that my own children would be deeply traumatized and my spouse would be miserable, that my father would be perplexed and my siblings hugely unsettled, what were my options?

Being transgender isn't a "choice" for anyone, and for me to have pretended to be a man for the rest of my life wasn't viable. Many people simply think transgender persons like me should go and get more therapy, or "man up" and deal with it. All I can say in response is that it just isn't like that. If it were, I'd have been there.

To be clear, I wasn't altogether unattached to being Stephen. I came to that realization in a moment of hard-edged clarity, when I was driving back from the Prince George's County Courthouse in Maryland having just filed the paperwork to become legally named Chloe. I had just obliterated my male name. I'd been so focused on all of the procedures and fees, timing and legalities, and so distracted by worries about how the clerks would react that I never stopped to think about what it might mean to me to no longer own the name of Stephen. I needn't have worried about the clerks; they acted as if this was a daily occurrence and went about the process with polite courtesy and efficiency. With a signature—a Chloe signature—I dumped my name.

The enormity of the demise of the name I'd used for five decades didn't hit me until I was halfway home from that transaction. It hit me hard; I had to pull over onto the shoulder and let the tears flow. No one seemed to notice me, the impersonal traffic flowed past, and I was alone in a way I hadn't ever quite experienced before. Amidst the tears I castigated myself for not having asked a friend to accompany me. A monumental threshold had been crossed, unwitnessed by anyone who cared for me. There would be other monumental moments on this journey, and each would be bittersweet, but this was the first. I stayed on that highway shoulder for a very long time, gradually picking up the lightness and feel of the new name, and wriggling back into it.

Chloe is who I am, and as such I am an interesting, happy, peace-filled, resilient, and loving person. Even through the copious tears, that fact of life was evident to me even then. In my distress I owned that authenticity, together with the satisfaction of having brought such a person into the lives of family and friends. For me, Chloe is worth it.

For others, the arrival of Chloe was not always warmly welcomed. It was quickly made clear to me that my decision—choice—to stay the course and transition gender was going to be turbulent and emotional for everyone concerned. "Everyone concerned" turned out to be a long list with my name at the top. I suppose I shouldn't have been so surprised; most people resist change, and the changes involved in transitioning deal with such delicate, complicated, and often unmentionable topics as sexuality and identity. These are no small matters. Transgender people pick up on this, and often put off the decision as long as possible. When that dam breaks, it does so with such intensity of thoughts and feelings that many outsiders misinterpret this as a radical life decision that is being rushed, or one that is irrational or bizarre—instead of simply being long overdue.

Short of postulating a sudden nervous breakdown, no one who knew me in the period leading up to 2006–2007 would have judged me irrational or heading for a major change of life. The reservoir behind my own dam was deep and large, and had been held back for such a long time. I'd managed to live my life as Stephen for more than half a century and by most external measures my life had been calm, successful and consistently rational. I had a loving family, an accomplished professional career, abundant academic qualifications, friends, comprehensive international experience, and a beautiful wife of remarkable caring, intelligence, and grace. Still, when the dam broke, the waters ran fast and strong.

Time and distance complicate any attempt now to explain the environment that led to that dam-breaking decision in 2007. I'm not even sure if the dam broke on its own, or if I had a hand in it. I now gaze back from such a different place; the peace and grounding I currently enjoy (and begin to take for granted, just a little) bears no comparison to the genuine angst, ever-building stress, and emptiness of pre-decision Stephen.

Putting the dam metaphor aside, I join with so many other transgender persons in often describing the experience of being wrongly embodied as a form of dissonance—akin to an irritating shrill noise that won't ever go away. Try as I might, I was never able to adjust to the irritation—the tinnitus of the soul—that grew louder and more insistent by the day. The phenomenon is poignantly private, given that society gets either squeamish or vindictive when men put on dresses. Even eliciting the empathy of others is largely impossible; it's like trying to describe to a man the fear, anguish, and growing intensity of the pain of childbirth. He may express sympathy and concern, but actually sensing that reality is outside his world. Being pregnant has an end date and a pregnant woman once pregnant doesn't exercise a very wide degree of choice about giving birth. Being afflicted by the unbearably growing dissonance of life in the wrong body arguably also has its narrowing choice of options over time. It certainly felt that way, and my due date was well past. Even after having made the decision to transition, almost everyone then urged me to go slowly, and they expressed considerable alarm at the rate of change they saw in me.

I had no intention of taking things slowly after so many years wrongly embodied. I wanted to sprint!

I'm a Quaker, and have no reticence in admitting to being a religious and spiritually grounded person. If most people were of little help to me at the outset of my transition, I wasn't finding a comforting reassurance from any divine sources either. There have been moments when I just knew that if there is a God, that God must have a very keen sense of irony (or a questionable sense of humor). Certainly I felt no divine sense of clarity or purpose in the long period leading up to my decision. All that I felt was pain, darkness, and emptiness—at many times excruciating and overwhelming.

I had sought help from the professionals, yet in 2006 I left my final appointment with my latest therapist, feeling utterly alone and confounded. I thought back despondently over the trail of final appointments with so many previous therapists, and the repeated and intensifying sense of frustration that not one of them seemed able to understand my "situation." Reflecting on this now, it was silly of me to have been so vexed with them—I hadn't any clear idea myself what was troubling me so completely. I just knew that my life was making no sense, that the deepest and most important relationships in my life were either troubled or hollow, and that I had no clear path before me. What therapist could unravel that?

So I stopped, or perhaps I simply failed to move on. Stopping sounds too much like a strong decision, and I was past making strong decisions. Instead, I found myself immobile (if physically safe) on a sidewalk near a very busy intersection in Silver Spring, Maryland, incapable of taking another step. Perhaps this paralysis was triggered by my latest bout of stinging self-criticism, as I judged myself lacking in both integrity and authenticity. I was an actor, playing the roles of husband, father, brother, son, nephew—all of the gendered roles in my life were approximations that significantly obscured the person behind the projections. I just didn't feel like I could continue the role-playing another day or even another hour, when all those who knew me in those roles weren't seeing the person within. But who was within? I'd never seen her in the mirror, except in faint but electrifying hints through certain fleeting facial expressions, or just once with the illicit aid of a furtive touch of makeup. As I stood amidst the noise and commotion on that sidewalk, I reflected on the irony that my graduate students viewed me as the professor who was teaching them all about ethics, integrity, and splendid theories of virtue, duty, caring, justice, and flourishing, yet to me my life was utterly devoid of integrity. I was living a fundamental and pervasive lie, but neither I nor any of the many therapists I'd relied upon to that date had been able to explain it, or had shown me any way to reconcile masculinity within my core identity.

In reflection, the explanation of that sidewalk state of mind is now clear: the dissonance had reached the point of being quite simply unbearable. At that low point I wasn't even thinking about making a choice to transition gender; that wasn't a coherent option to me. All I knew was that my life was hollow and not worth living, but no words were available to explain why, even to myself. There on that sidewalk all that remained to me, as the impersonal torrent of rush-hour traffic surged past me, was the sharp-edged clarity that one choice did remain within my power. I'd never even approached that point of clarity before: there was a way out, the ultimate way out. That thought alone shook me deeply, but then unexpectedly a calm settled over me as I perceived how irrefutably sensible that choice was. All that remained was to decide when and how to exercise my choice.

Over time the memory of that existential moment has dulled, even if the pain lingers. Thankfully, that terrible moment no longer threatens me. The drama of that suicidal intention on the sidewalk has long since lost its edge, as the reasons behind that awful choice were themselves swept aside by subsequent events, and by one particular door opening. Or to be more precise, by fulfilling one promise. I'd agreed to a friend's recommendation that I see yet one more therapist—one whom she had enthusiastically recommended. Even though I was past the point of believing that any therapist would be able to offer any light or hope, I'd made that promise. I chose to fulfill that obligation quickly, get it behind me, and then be ready to attend to that final resolution.

On the appointed day, not long after my existential sidewalk choice had been made, I calmly entered Jenn Hackler's office free from the burden of expectations. The appointment went along as had all the others before, save only that this therapist listened to me with a remarkable intensity. The forty minutes flew past as I drew close to the point in my narrative in which I described the total cacophony and lack of cohesion at my center, and my pervasive uneasiness with the maleness that I felt throughout my body. She seemed more curious than moved. Fixing me with a kindly but intense stare, she asked just one question.

"Well, did you ever stop to think you might be a woman?"

Looking back, the logic of her question is obvious. At the time, it was revelatory. I'd never dared to ask myself that question, nor had I ever approached that point of self-honesty. The transcendent truth behind the question overwhelmed me like no question ever had, and just the possibility that a person of knowledge and perception would have the calm audacity—the simplicity—to ask that question utterly changed my world. More memorable still is my mental image as her question took root: the sense of a very large, tall, ugly, unbalanced, and complex structure shifting radically, amidst much dust and clamor. In its place there emerged something still large, tall and complex, yet orderly—even beautiful, and resplendent of light and grace. The earlier momentous sidewalk decision instantly became somehow quaint, from someone else's life; still the immensity of her question left me shaking as I contemplated its implications and felt its weighty truth.

She concluded the appointment by explaining that perhaps I was transgender, while being quick to qualify that opinion by acknowledging that she had no particular expertise in treating people with this condition. She directed me to a therapist who worked only on transgender issues: Martha Harris, of the Banyan Counseling Center in Alexandria,

Virginia. In the weeks and months that followed, Martha calmly and expertly led me through a rigorous diagnostic process, opening my eyes to what she could see all too plainly.

I was indeed a woman, neither by choice nor decision. A transgender woman. I just needed to own that.

TESTING FRIENDSHIPS

Victoria's response was unequivocal. "Wow! Congratulations!" Her eyes gleamed with affirmation.

That spontaneous response, coming from Vic, meant the world to me. Vic—a Canadian American—is one of those few and very special kindred spirits whose presence on the global stage (often in locations that only people with similarly bizarre resumes find their way to) somehow validates my own "exotic" career path, or confirms that we're both unrepentant idiots together. We're sisters in the international development and humanitarian relief game, and that entails taking risks that most of our fellow citizens would balk at. They're right to balk—we've worked in absurdly dangerous places. I've done my time in Somalia, in Sudan and South Sudan, the Gaza Strip, in Uganda during a civil war, and in El Salvador during a very uneasy truce. Vic's worked helping refugees and internally displaced persons in the turbulent and violent city of Peshawar in Pakistan, in the war-torn country of Yemen, in some of the roughest parts of Nigeria, Egypt, and Lebanon, and soon she'll be moving to work in the city of Adana in southeast Turkey, close to the Syrian border. She's tough, feminine, intelligent, beautiful, resourceful, and courageous, and she is a friend whose assessment I value greatly.

There, at a cheesecake joint in Friendship Heights, she sat in rapt attention as I shared my news. The restaurant booth felt safe in an anonymous way, and her presence opposite me was reassuring. She was the very first person besides my wife Christine to whom I came out, and her unrehearsed response was wonderful, caring, and—to be sure—not at all what I'd dared to hope for. Even though I considered her to be a dear friend, I'd prepared myself for shock, disbelief, unease, perhaps even some well-intended humor. Instead, I was deeply buoyed by her broad smile and sparkling eyes. Vic's immediate and complete acceptance of my coming out was the sincere and unrehearsed gift of a friend, to be cherished forever.

In those early, awkward days and prior to making my public announcement, I didn't have many friends to whom I could come out, or share with regarding my intentions to transition. That scarcity was much more a product of my own insecurities and sense of vulnerability than the capacity of any of my closest friends to hear and respond supportively to this news. After Vic, among the very few with whom I did share this news one common reaction was their admission that they'd always harbored a suspicion that I was a closeted gay man. Every time I heard that it astounded me; I really didn't know what to say. Sexual orientation for me had always been heterosexual, but transitioning gender raises havoc with such classifications. Was I going to transition from a heterosexual male into a lesbian? I assumed so, but it wasn't clear. Still, from my perspective the "gay man" label simply never fit me.

Gay or straight, the bigger and more imposing challenge was that Stephen had been replaced by an upstart, a so-called woman who called herself Chloe. Not all friends were warm to this new incarnation from the outset. In the spring of 2009, Mary Joel, my friend of many years, waited for me at the top of the Bethesda Metro Station in the Washington, DC, suburbs. She'd yet to see me as Chloe, and she admitted to me later she'd been nervous at that prospect. Would I look awkward? Would it be embarrassing to be seen with me? Was I going to talk or act irrationally? Would my voice be uncomfortably masculine? Fortunately, the emergence of the reality of Chloe at the top of the escalator vanquished those fears. The waitress addressed us as "ladies" (which I still to this day get a thrill from, even after all these years). As we talked over lunch and moved beyond momentary anxieties and pleasantries, Mary Joel needed to know why I'd chosen to do such a thing. It's the right question, but it also begs another question in the asking. Was my decision to journey across the gender divide a choice, or a necessity?

The questions about that journey were simply too big, too threatening, too radical, and too complicated—right from the outset. Where should I go for help? Who should I avoid? Which of my friends or family should I wait to tell until "the decision" was already made? Should I share how acutely vulnerable I felt? Should I communicate in a way that spoke to the clarity and steely conviction that this path was my only plausible way forward, and let them know that what I was really asking them for wasn't their blessing or even their advice, but their support? Or at least their forbearance.

I didn't really know.

Everywhere I looked, objectivity, knowledge, and understanding were in very short supply. Everyone had some stake in me staying Stephen, and I sensed that even trusted mentors and those within the ranks of family, friends, and coworkers would be unnerved if I sought their advice. But I really needed help, even though I knew that many whom I approached would push back, reflexively, and with vigor. And many did. A small hate mail collection began, and it grew. Most such messages were more of indignity than hate, but two were filled with vitriol, anger, and outrage. Neither author ever wrote to me later to retract any of their comments, even the ones that seemed truly venomous. I still have the letters, stuffed some-where in a box. I will burn them someday soon, when I'm ready.

While my closest friends stood by me, not all the people whom I considered friends—or at least friendly acquaintances—were as sponta-neously gracious when they learned I was transgender. There were em-phatically angry responses too, but these had their origins in fear and ignorance of the transgender phenomenon. Their fury was further fueled by their conviction that I was willfully, callously, and selfishly pursuing this path while blithely disregarding the welfare of my immediate family. In some instances, the friendship was deep enough to allow for an ex-change—a chance to build understanding and to reassure them that the interests of my then wife and my children were uppermost in my mind and that as a tight family we were working this through together. Still, even after some direct contacts, most of those friends whose immediate reactions had been harshly negative were only partially mollified—from anger to profound misgivings. Some relented when they saw Christine and me still together and engaged in our normal lives. That witness of our constancy as a couple persuaded them that her understanding and acceptance were real, and that the best hope for my family and for me was to trust in Christine's assessment that my decision to transition had been existential, not optional.

Other friends were more befuddled than upset or angry. On the after-noon of my fortieth high school reunion, as Christine and I settled into our hotel room in Potsdam, in the far northern part of New York State, my old high school buddy Stanley came to call. Stanley is authentic "North Country"—the product of a life in largely rural St. Lawrence County, where concepts like "political correctness" are thin and where knowledge of the transgender phenomenon is scarce. He entered the room with more hesitation than was his norm, not taking his eyes off of me as I sat in the gold-upholstered Louis XVI–style armchair by the window, feeling pretty. Christine sat in the matching chair, also looking her best, and together in that florid yellow-wallpapered, well-appointed room we probably formed a very convincing portrait of refined femininity. This was hardly a normal Potsdam scene he found himself in. Seeing no chair available, he made a space for himself on the bed in our hotel room where he sat stiffly, eyes as big as saucers. At first he just sat and stared, taking in this woman who at one time had been one of his best high school male friends. My dear old buddy Stan was clearly struggling to make sense of the enigma of Chloe— the struggle was written all over his face, even if his smile remained warm and reassuring. Stan was never one to hold back; with a clearing of his throat he asked what "this" was all about, and did I intend to stay this way. It was not a disapproving or critical question, but it was intense, and it was sincere. He asked if changing genders was even possible, short of losing one's sanity. In fact, he asked a lot of questions, not all of them "genteel." I'd never known Stan to attend to polite niceties when he didn't feel re-quired to, so while a little taken aback I wasn't offended at his frank eager-ness to know if I had already "had it cut off!" I explained, with a calmness that surprised me, that I had not yet taken that big step, and that "cutting it off" wasn't really an apt description of what gender confirming surgery consisted of anyway. Before he could even catch his breath I was prompt to add, however, that I could barely wait until I could save the large sum of money needed to undergo such a procedure. He was astounded, almost dumbstruck. After collecting himself, he owned the truth that my disclo-sure had made him physically cringe. Again he asked after my sanity, but again with his constant warm smile, and a look to Christine perhaps for confirmation that this wasn't all some crazy theatrical event. Stanley was confounded, and it was clear beyond any doubt that my presence in a dress (even a pretty one) wasn't a reality he was ready to embrace—especially right there in Potsdam, the town where we both had forged so many high school memories. Oddly, I wasn't chagrined by his unwillingness to buy into Chloe, and to let Stephen go. After all, this was Stan, a very special person in my life, and as far as I was concerned there were no wrong questions. He mused and stretched, told a joke or two, and—in true Stanley form—asked me if I now had the hots for him! I don't think he was disappointed when I laughed and answered in the negative.

Despite anything I could offer him then in the way of explanation, Stan just didn't get it. That evening at the class reunion, however, the man whom I had always admired and cherished as the closest of friends showed up, in more ways than filling a space. Stan stood by my side with the loyalty and caring that I'd always treasured him for, but now also with a protectiveness that I found strangely comforting, if unexpected. Not everyone at the evening gathering was happy to see Chloe; one former female classmate in particular could only speak in the snarkiest of terms about "very confused men in the wrong places" as we waited in the ladies' room to dry our hands amidst a gaggle of our former female classmates. Still, with both Stan and my then wife beside me at the table, I exulted in their sheltering bubble. In some ways, I felt a bigger challenge being there in Potsdam when the heavy-set male classmate sitting at our table, whom I did not recall at all from high school days and who never once showed any signs of recognizing my transgender status, proudly chose to show off his photo album. He drew my particular attention to a photo of his granddaughter cradling the rifle he'd recently bought her as her eleventh birthday present. His NRA lapel pin sparkled as he crinkled his face in a broad smile of grandfatherly delight. The values, politics, and daily realities that this rough but caring family man exemplified were from a world that was no longer my world in many important ways. Perhaps it never really had been. Potsdam suddenly felt more alien and remote than it ever had before, and my history as Stephen in that town took on an air of un-reality that I struggled to reconcile.

Stan, however, took no reconciliation. He was and remains my friend, and he was attentive to me throughout the evening. When I looked across the banquet table at him, I remembered well those unsettling high school years when he and I both had been affable outcasts in our own ways. Al-ways a straight and witty talker and a loyal friend, he hadn't balked when I urged him in 1968 to join with me in signing up for the sewing class. We became the first two boys ever to take that class in Potsdam Central High School, enduring the giggles and marginally hostile stares of our female classmates. Together, Stan and I had retained our composure when the teacher had asked us to step out into the corridor so that she could talk to the rest of the class about "foundations." Sewing was creating, and he and I loved to make things. I don't recall what garments he made, but I made a bikini for my then girlfriend (which included a discreet—but enjoyable—fitting session) and then later I made her prom dress, which she was gracious enough to wear (It wasn't really that bad!). At the end of that academic year, Stan went on to share with me the prize at the school awards ceremony for having attained the two highest grades in the sewing class. The entire school body struggled with whether to laugh or to be qui-etly impressed as we both walked up to the stage to accept the prize. Only the presence of so many teachers kept the snickers at bay, yet one thing I am sure of is that both Stan and I were proud to have won that accolade. I still enjoy sewing when I can find the time, but I haven't had the cheeki-ness to ask Stan if he still does.

I thought about Stan a lot that night. Where I had been a sensitive and subdued teen—perhaps my way of expressing femininity—Stan had been boisterous, popular, and a clown. He always had a story ready, and the wild tales of his French Canadian uncle, "Black Bob," were probably mostly made up, but no one cared. They were terrific tales. For my part, I immersed myself in scholarship, and could think of no better way of spending a lunch hour than in the library, fascinated (if a little bewildered) by the powerfully masculine tales of Greek mythology, or the softly feminine respite that poetry offered. I don't recall ever seeing Stan in that library. Where I was at best marginally athletic, Stan was a jock. I watched him from the bleachers with admiration as "Stan the Man" played on the school's basketball team, and cheered him on as he also excelled on the track team. I surprised myself in not feeling any envy when he started dating my best female friend, Annette, other than chagrin that he cut into my time on the phone with her. Stan, and our other mutual friend Peter who was a year older, both enjoyed one high school romance after another with girls I knew, with teen-significant drama at almost every turn. Throughout, I was the quiet spectator, the reliable designated driver, never quite sure what to make of high school girls as potential romantic (much less sexual) partners. Other than befriending many of them in platonic but close relationships, I left the dating to Stan and Pete.

That night at the reunion Stan looked healthy and fit, sitting at our table. That was very gratifying to see; he had fallen victim to a terrible summer job–related explosion in 1969 and had been rushed off by helicopter to the state's best burn unit in Albany. Every weekend that followed, I'd jumped aboard my Honda CB 350 motorcycle and ridden the three hours across the Adirondack Mountains to see him. Through fortitude and strength of character, Stan had defied the odds and all the doctors' prognoses. He had clawed his way back to health, although it took many months. The extent of his injuries shook me deeply when I first began those visits, but I had never doubted for a moment that he would bounce back. I was always eager each weekend to climb aboard that motorcycle to drive to Albany and back; he was that kind of a friend. Being by his side was the best I could offer, but offer it I did, along with the watermelons I somehow strapped to the carrier rack of my motorcycle. And there I was again, at his side and he by mine, as the reunion night festivities continued. This time, there was no watermelon, and no deep-throated roar of a motorcycle.

Over the many years since high school I'd barely kept up any communication with Stan, especially during those long years when I was in Africa, but on the rare occasions when we did meet again it always felt like we were picking up a colorful (and sometimes off-color) conversation from the day before. But not when Stan first met me as Chloe; the conversation had no precedent. Stephen (or "Steve" as he would have called me) wasn't there, and Chloe was a mystery. To his credit, while he never appeared to grasp the reasons for my transition, he did what good friends do—he defaulted to trusting in a friend. It was a genuine gift, and I remain thankful to him. After a short time into that reunion it wasn't our gender differences but our significant divergence in political views that became far more challenging to our shared friendship. No doubt we'd overcome that too, or find a way to agree to keep our political views to ourselves, if we were to spend more time together.

Not everyone in my life made the transition with me, but most of the ones who fell by the wayside did so quietly. Others found a new reason to reconnect, and to build a stronger friendship. Some who had been close but who had moved in different directions in their lives communicated their support, if not their understanding. In particular, I remember Stan and my late friend Pete, who had passed away much too young. After high school, Pete had gone on to fly helicopters for the Army in Vietnam, and then he'd pursued a life as a helicopter test pilot for Boeing. The few times I saw him over the years, I was aware of how turbulent his life was as he fought against the substance abuse that had consumed both his parents, and now threatened his two younger sisters. With his parents largely incapacitated by alcoholism, his Norwegian grandmother Anna Maria Nelson raised him and his three sisters, and I too benefitted from her caring, strong example of womanhood. When I knew her in the late 1960s and early 1970s, she was already quite elderly, but she exuded a strength and permanence that was the bedrock of that family. I would sit quite literally at her feet whenever the opportunity presented itself, transfixed by her detailed accounts of her girlhood in rural Norway at the turn of the century, where she had rowed a boat to school every day. She spoke also of her emigration first to Canada at the age of seventeen, and her later move with her husband Harold to New York State. As she would recount her adventures, her hands would always be busy. She knit beautiful double-knit Scandinavian mittens, sweaters, and hats with incredibly intricate patterns. She created beautiful quilts and gave me one that I used for years until it was threadbare. She even had a loom set up on the back porch where she would weave rugs. She also made braided rugs and hooked rugs, and did embroidery and hardanger work. Her industriousness and strength of character, as well as her grace and wisdom, live on in Pete's oldest sister, Ann McGowan.

After Pete left his modest family home in Potsdam, the Army had provided him with some clear boundaries and a strong sense of purpose, shaping him into a man of determination and accomplishment. His military demeanor and toughness always had a soft spot that I could reach, however. In his late fifties he had moved to Alabama, and there was no prospect of being able to spend time with him there as Chloe. A letter would have to do, although I knew that it would hardly be adequate. When he received my letter with the news of my transition, he courteously asked me by email for some time to digest the news and reflect on it. He ended his message by saying: "I want you to know that, regardless of your chosen gender (and it is your choice), you will always have my brotherly love and support." It was a sentence that came back to me again and again as I attended his funeral at the red sandstone Trinity Episcopal Church on Fall Island in Potsdam, where years before we had been members of the Episcopal Young Churchmen—the organization of Episcopal teens. I smiled just a little as I felt his lingering presence in that church, secure in the knowledge that Pete would have liked Chloe.

There was also another Peter whom I've known since high school, but unlike my late friend, this Peter was never particularly close to me when I was young. I had liked him from a distance, however, and he had always been unfailingly polite and civil—not necessarily common virtues among high school classmates. Even though he and his wife, Ann, went on to pursue a similar international life as mine, we barely stayed in contact before my transition. Something about my journey, however, seems to have been a catalyst for better communication, and since 2008 we've found a friendship of mutual respect, caring, and common ground. Peter is among my most faithful Facebook friends, and one of the few people I know on that medium who can communicate with true feeling, wry humor, stunning photographs of Vermont, and even words of wisdom and deep insight. When my daughter Audrey and I visited Peter and Ann at their lovely home in Middlebury, we talked and talked. Their complete acceptance of me as a friend and as a woman was unquestionable, and that warm embrace felt like a precious and unselfconscious validation of me as Chloe in ways that my daughter certainly seemed to register. The affection that Peter and Ann showed me then feels very tangible, and we will remain close friends in the years ahead. Indeed, my presence in their lives as Chloe has opened a door to that friendship in ways that would have been improbable before. Every time that I think of Peter and Ann feels like a cherished invitation that awaits my further response.

I've lived much of my adult life in Africa or the United Kingdom, and have friends of diverse cultural and national backgrounds. I wondered how some of them would take the news of my transition. I really needn't have worried; in nearly every case they were wonderful. My British friends Joanna and Bill could not be a better example. When I had first met them back in the 1980s, they had seemed like they'd wandered off of a film set about life in colonial Kenya. It wasn't just their accents; Bill worked as the senior accountant for a British tea company, and they lived in a large stone house in the genteel outskirts of Nairobi, set on elegantly manicured lawns among resplendent ambassadorial residences. When I met them as Chloe, they had long since returned to live in Birmingham, England, where they welcomed me with warm smiles and without fuss. Their affection was as genuine as my identity. I stayed with them for a weekend layover en route from Africa back to the United States, and our conversations were vibrant. We discussed Bill's project to write a book about elder abuse, from the poignant perspective of the tragic way in which his own mother had been treated by a paid caregiver. The intensity of that conversation and the trust that they both showed in me to share such deeply personal experiences made the fact of my gender transition almost irrelevant—and delightfully so. With them, the awkward questions about how my transition was being received by the many people in my life, and what I thought and felt as a "new" woman in the world, weren't awkward at all. These were the questions of friends who genuinely care about me and wish me well, and I left that weekend knowing I had the same friends as Chloe as I had ever had before.

I also had a chance to spend some time in Tanzania with a dear East African friend named Kaisi. He and I go way back; he worked with me when I established my Nairobi architectural firm, Landplan Group Africa. In time he left Kenya to set up and run a new branch office in Dar es Salaam, Tanzania, of which he and a woman architect now share ownership. The firm is now both an architectural practice called Landplan-Icon Architects, as well as a design-build development practice called Mutual Developers Limited, and together it's one of the largest and most successful architectural and development practices in the country. The first and only time that I've had the opportunity to visit him as Chloe, he took me to the firm (which I no longer have any formal ties to) and introduced me to his staff as "the mother of the firm!" I could not have felt more proud, touched, or respected. Kaisi continues to phone me from time to time as the spirit moves him, and his phone calls are so special to me. He is a rare and dear soul—an opinion I know I am not alone in holding.

Another key figure from the Landplan chapter of my life is Bharat, an Indian architect whom I met at my very first job in Nairobi with a local architectural firm; our drawing boards were in close proximity, and lively conversation filled the space between us. We became and stayed firm friends, and he participated in the beginnings of Landplan. We even went to jail together (the mark of true friends if ever there was one) in Uganda in a frightening saga that could've easily ended much worse. We became victims of the revenge of a well-connected, sleazy building contractor whose contract we had cancelled due to his corruption and nonperformance. Before that incident, Bharat had bravely volunteered to establish Landplan's branch office in Kampala, Uganda, and such incidents at that time weren't uncommon in the turbulence of that post-conflict nation. That he and his wife Asha endured such hardships took considerable courage and no small degree of sacrifice. He's since closed that office and returned with his wife to retire first in India, and later in Florida, but he did find some time to meet me at my office during a family visit to Washington, DC, in 2011. It was clear to me that he had to lay eyes on me to let my news make sense to him, much more than ask me any specific questions. After some time together he looked at me long and hard, sighed audibly, and said: "Well, that took balls!" I was quick to assure him that balls were the one thing that I'd needed least in my transition.

Also harkening to my many roots in Africa, Peter and Maggie are a British couple I knew well when I lived in Nairobi. For many years I had lost contact with them, even to the point of visiting their old residence in Karen (just outside Nairobi) and having the eerie "parallel universe" experience of going to the place in their former property's perimeter wall where the gate had been, only to see that the opening had been closed up with no trace remaining that it had ever existed (the gate having been relocated to another side of the property by the new owner). That experience rattled me, and the drive back into Nairobi felt empty and surreal. In time, however, and thanks to the Internet, I was able to track them down. In 2014, I found an opportunity to visit them in Nairobi; they were both absolutely thrilled to see me. In very short order they decided that I was definitely "genuine" and that my persona as Chloe conveyed a femininity that was persuasive and authentic across all dimensions! Peter is a ladies' man, at least in spirit, and it felt initially curious and then just amusing to watch his eyes as he took me in—his eyes rediscovered my face just before it got too silly. Maggie is a woman who enjoys socializing with women, and she promptly launched into girl talk in a way that felt at first like a probe of my "qualifications" but quickly turned into an engaging and fun conversation. Finding the delight in girl talk has been a continued blessing since my transition, and that night was no exception. Having got that initial (but endearing) set of inspections and interrogations out of the way right there in the entry lobby of the restaurant in one of Nairobi's new and upscale shopping precincts, we were shown our way to the candle-lit table in the crowded but still intimate main dining room. A threshold had been passed almost effortlessly, it seemed to me, and we spent the rest of that evening dining on a delicious Italian meal and drinking far too much wine, with Peter telling the rudely hysterical jokes he is known for, and both of them carrying on with me without the slightest discomfort. From all I could tell in the way that they embraced me with hugs, words, and smiles, they had always been friends with Chloe. Yes, there were some mentions of old exploits from some of our safaris across remote areas of Kenya, and they seemed quite at ease in making comments such as "when you were Stephen" and moving on with the conversation, almost as if such gender changes were commonplace. It was a wonderful evening, and something tells me there will be more like it in upcoming trips. Peter is one of the best-informed Brits in Kenya when it comes to going camping, a pastime which, ironically, Maggie cannot abide. I delight in memories of camping safaris with Peter and a few other friends on numerous occasions back in the 1980s, episodes made memorable by always awakening to the early morning smell of bacon cooking on a campfire. Peter was always eager for another day "in the bush," and used his morning-person inclinations to get us all up and moving by appealing to our stomachs. No expatriate I know has ever derived so much pleasure out of a day in the African countryside as Peter, and I would seize any opportunity to join him in yet another camping safari, even if I have long since given up eating bacon!

Another long-standing friend, and a woman whom I deeply admire for her gumption and success in achieving a masterful senior executive role in the tough and male-dominated world of international engineering, is Julie. Attractive, buoyant, competent in the extreme, filled with ideas, irritatingly Republican, and always delightfully feminine even when she's swearing at folks, Julie is and always has been indomitable. She and her very attentive, caring, handsome, and fabulous husband Dave have stood by me from the start of my transition. That "start" for Julie became much more tangible when I invited her to lunch in Washington at a busy restaurant crowded with office workers and executives, intending to give her a chance to settle into me as Chloe. Her face was quite simply aglow with delight in "meeting" Chloe, and she took it all in stride but went even further. Julie was effusive in her compliments, such as observing in passing that my choice of lipstick (L'Oreal Ginger Spice 815) was terrific, and how perfect it was for my complexion. It was the boost that I needed from an elegant and attractive woman I deeply admire. After we went our separate ways following lunch, I went out and immediately bought three more of the same lipstick. Affirmation is a powerful elixir. Julie and her husband Dave remain among my closest friends, even if they are physically remote in their picturesque and historical country house in Madison, Virginia. My many visits to see them are universally delightful, validating, and fun—and I was even persuaded by them to help their firm in doing a two-week consulting assignment in Kabul, Afghanistan, where I had my first chance not only to wear a hijab, but also body armor. Only Julie could have talked me into that!

There are also more than a few of my relatives whom I count among my most stalwart friends, in particular my first cousins Sue, Judy, Dottie, and Stephanie. They each were immediately responsive in a strongly supportive way when they first received my coming-out announcement. Each woman and their husbands have supported me in the most challenging moments, and have made the effort to stay in communication. My transition drew me much closer to each of them.

I also now have a new category of friends and close acquaintances: people who've only known me as Chloe. Thankfully that's a growing category and a less complicated set of relationships to navigate; when they look at me they only see one person and not a before/after. These newer friends offer me a valued opportunity to move ahead in my life as a woman, building friendships that are largely unencumbered by a complicated history. Some are coworkers, some are from my Quaker community, and some are people I've met along the way, but each is valued. They range in age from fifteen to well above seventy years old, of all genders, and from a variety of backgrounds. What's particularly satisfying for me is to simply be present with them, and see how the space between us fills with shared conversations and mutual experiences. There's never any need to strain for a conversation; my Chloe self has much to say and no problem expressing it! Perhaps that facility with easy discourse is a *girl thing*, but I don't need to label it—just enjoy it as a gift.

In various ways, and to varying degrees, all of my friendships have been tested by the reality that I am a transgender woman, sometimes referred to as a transsexual[2]—a woman with an "interesting," if confusing, history. Most of my friends found their own respective ways to incorporate that reality into our relationship and move on, in most cases making our relationships even closer and tighter in ways that would have been inconceivable before my transition. Some friends were not able to transition as I had and accommodate this new woman; by their own volition they are left only with their fading memories of Stephen. A few friends are still unsure, still somewhat remote, yet still wanting to remain connected—even if unable or unwilling to renegotiate the parameters of our friendships. Yet.

Coming out to my friends has been a steep hill to climb, but climb it I did. Traversing the mountain of coming out to my family was a far greater challenge.

---

2. "Transsexual" is a term that seems to be gradually falling out of favor. According to the Oxford English Dictionary, it refers to "persons who have undergone treatment in order to acquire the physical characteristics of the opposite sex," i.e., gender identity that is different than the gender identity and sex they were assigned at birth. I used to describe myself as a transsexual, but see no reason to do so now—as with many people, I now consider this term (as commonly understood) to be too clinical.

APPROACHING SISTERHOOD

Photograph by Christine Lucas

STARTING IN THE THIRD BASEMENT

Being two people at once isn't easy.

On certain workdays every two weeks, my strategy for attending appointments with my therapist was to park the car at the farthest corner of the lowest level of the three-level underground parking lot, away from all of the other cars. While not entirely dark, it was far from a bright place, and had I been thinking more clearly I probably wouldn't have been quite so obvious in being so intentionally remote. Still, the small Ford was my traveling changing room, and the last thing I wanted anyone to witness was my sartorial transformation from Stephen to Chloe, and then back again. Transforming myself in the back seat of a Ford Focus was no small accomplishment, although to me it never felt like cross-dressing; getting into feminine garb was more like stepping into myself.

The fortnightly fifteen-mile drive through city traffic from my office in the Friendship Heights region of Washington, DC, to Martha Harris, my gender-transition therapist in the outskirts of Alexandria, Virginia, took nearly an hour each way, but once I was suitably clothed, wigged, made up, in my Chloe mindset, and had put some distance between me and the office, the journey was a delight. The sense of liberation, freedom, and presence was palpable, and just being out in the world as Chloe—while somewhat protected from scrutiny wrapped in the safety of my car—was empowering, now that any anxiety of being found out (or "clocked," as some transgender folks will say) was negligible. The drive back to the office, and the prospect of putting the boy clothes back on, wasn't quite as bright.

On one occasion in early September of 2008 when I returned to the parking garage, I decided to indulge myself by running a small errand before returning into boy garb. As I walked from the garage along a long, well-lit, narrow, underground corridor I saw my boss approaching—a boss who knew nothing about Chloe. Surely this was going to be very awkward; there wasn't a thing to do but to keep on walking ahead, eyes forward, chin up. My boss passed me without a break in her stride or a glance in my direction. The feeling was nothing short of exultant, and timely too; shortly after that encounter I wrote to Wendy, the human resources officer at the firm, to inform her that as of September 3, 2008, my name had been legally changed to Chloe, and that as of Sunday, September 21, I would begin my gender transition. I formally asked that they assist me as would be appropriate in that process. I was "out." On Monday, September 22, Chloe would arrive at work. Being selectively out wasn't an option for me, so when I came out at work I came out to everyone who knew me.

Wendy was very understanding, empathetic, and professional—although quick to admit that she'd never encountered this situation before. When she raised this matter with the owner-managers of the firm, however, it was clear that her more difficult task would be to make them understand this situation in a positive way. The firm is owned and led by members of a traditional Roman Catholic family originally from South America, and my transition intentions left them in a very uncomfortable position relative to their own values, beliefs, and experiences. It was very quickly made clear to me that I was not to address this topic with any of them directly, and that all communications should be through the HR officer. That suited me, although it took considerable back-and-forth and numerous edits before the text of an announcement from me to the staff was agreed upon with Wendy, and via Wendy with the owners of the firm. That email message was as follows:

Sent: Wednesday, September 17, 2008 2:47 p.m.

Subject: a personal and significant update

Dear Friends and Colleagues,

My apologies for the "mass mailer," but it is time that I let you know about a change that is taking place within my life, and the life of my family. After a very long process of therapeutic evaluation and introspection, I have come into the clear knowledge that I am a transgender person. In short, I have a relatively rare neurobiological condition best summed up by the clinical fact that I have a woman's brain in a man's body. There is only one known cure—to bring my body into alignment with my brain. "Stephen" is therefore transitioning to become "Chloe," and I am already engaged in that process. Starting this Sunday, September 21, I will live my life as Chloe Schwenke.

I hope that this news does not distress you. I have found as I have shared this news with a few of those near to me that reactions differ greatly. Some are immediately warm and accepting. Others are afraid, even angry. For others still, the revelation brings up uncomfortable or unresolved issues in their own lives; they are confused and a bit bewildered, and simply don't know how to disentangle the many feelings and thoughts. All of these responses are natural. Gender is fundamental to our identity, and there are exceptionally strong forces unleashed in us all when the gender divide is compromised.

My wife and I have found a solid base of support from family and friends, and my wife Christine has been both understanding and unfailingly supportive of me as

I pursue this transition. Yet even among those close to us, many misunderstandings surround this transition. Gender identity gets confused with sexual orientation or cross-dressing, which are entirely separate sets of issues. Many people assume that when a person changes gender, their sexual orientation changes automatically. In reality, these are not directly linked. Others think of this transition as a "lifestyle" choice. Being authentic—being the person you really are—is certainly not reducible to a lifestyle. There are others still who think such a transition is an option. You must trust me; I would never take this arduous path were both my wife and I not clear that it was needed. It would also be irrational to choose to change one's gender unless no other cure was available, or one was mistaken in the diagnosis. There is no other cure, and the diagnosis is not in doubt.

Please feel free to ask me any questions. This is new territory for most people, and I am happy to respond to any appropriate question. (I'll tell you if we think a question is too personal!) I can also suggest some good books on the issue.

Finally, please do try to use my new (and now legal) proper name and pronouns. Of course I will be very forgiving of mistakes, and they are inevitable, but every time I hear "Chloe," "she," or "her," it speaks to me of acceptance and caring.

Warmly,

Chloe Schwenke

I used almost the identical email message to let the larger network of friends and contacts know this news, although close family members received separate and far more detailed letters. The reactions from my coworkers and larger network were generally positive, although no doubt the results were skewed. Those with less favorable views probably didn't feel inclined to respond at all to my message. Some expressed their happiness that I'd found a diagnosis and a path that would allow me inner peace. Others acknowledged that they were struggling to relate to what my personal state of mind and spirit must be to lead to such an outcome, but they nevertheless offered their full support. One perceptive friend recognized that the challenge for others would be accommodating these changes, while for me the world would still look the same, at least visually. "The issue is in our eyes," he said. Another jauntier response was refreshingly straightforward: "I am behind you one hundred percent. Let's have lunch!"

Helping my friends to understand while hopefully eliciting their support was a very different exercise than navigating the multitude of differing relationships that comprised my office environment during my gender transition. As I explained to the HR officer, Wendy, the logistics of explaining my transition in understandable language to an office staff of over 120 persons of many nationalities was daunting. I proposed to her that just before I stopped dressing as Stephen I should hold a very matter-of-fact meeting for all who were interested to come and find out more, ask their questions, and come to their own conclusion about how best to move forward. The HR officer was very supportive of this idea, and she offered to co-host the gathering so that issues of corporate policy, inclusion, my use of the women's restroom, and other similarly earth-shaking matters could be addressed. The firm's management resisted, however, taking the view that my transition was a personal issue and not something appropriate to discuss in an office meeting. After some considerable back-and-forth through the good efforts of the HR officer, it was finally agreed that I could hold the meeting immediately after office hours. Invitations were therefore sent out for a 5:00 p.m. meeting on the last Thursday of my Stephen-hood, and the vast majority of those invited responded that they were coming. But at 4:45 p.m. on that Thursday, as I nervously tried to think through how best to discuss all of this, word came down from management (quite literally—they were a floor above me) that the meeting was cancelled. My boss decided that no such meeting would be held within the premises of the firm. I was informed that if I chose to rent a room outside of the firm that could hold that many people, I'd be welcome to invite the staff—after working hours of course. Obviously no such meeting was personally affordable, and hence no meeting was ever held.

The only consolation came when most of the African-American women of the firm squeezed into my small office the next day, closed the door, and informed me that no matter what the boss had said they wanted the scoop. These ladies were pushy, assertive, bold, and full of warm smiles. With so many gathered, there was barely any room to move in that small office, but they stood patiently while I collected my thoughts. I stumbled at first as I spoke, but they were warm and supportive as I did my best to explain the reasons why this would soon be Chloe's office. I explained—well, made the case—that my transition was something that nearly all transgender persons feel a deep compulsion to undergo—that this is not a choice or a "lifestyle." Some of their faces softened, accommodating this notion, and a few shed some tears. Others continued to smile, but in a way that allowed their doubts to be evident. If it hadn't been for the sincerity of their smiles, I would have felt like I was being held in judgment. There was inevitably some degree of that going on; several of these women came from strongly evangelical backgrounds that made no room for the transgender phenomenon, and their initial reactions had been ones of stern disapproval. Still, the smiles were all that mattered to me, and my smiles in response gave them the permission they needed to take the conversation where they wanted it to go. They asked all the naughty questions, such as how my wife was coping with a husband who was becoming a woman. Did we still sleep together? Were we still intimate—and would we stay that way? Did I fancy any of the men in the firm? Or was I going to be a lesbian? It amused them when I said that I really didn't know who

I fancied, or how I would renegotiate the intimate relationship in my life—all of these things would become clear in their own time. Loud laughs ensued, and one woman declared that she too was trying to sort that out in her own life. The laughs grew louder, until one woman wanted to know if I had scheduled my surgery. At her question, the room went suddenly silent, as I admitted that I hadn't. They heard me say that I was certainly looking into it, and they saw my grimace as I acknowledged that I had no plan for how I'd ever afford it. The interrogation was suddenly over, but the kindly stares continued for a moment. I felt like I had given them what they needed to know, and that they were persuaded by what I had shared. As they left, each offered me her best wishes, and their consistent smiles in the weeks ahead sustained me. Their initiative in finding their own ways to come to terms with my change, and simultaneously make me welcome in their world, was the highpoint of my last week of being Stephen. My small office felt to me like it had been transformed by their presence.

I won't pretend that arriving at work that following Monday was a calm experience, but my awareness of a fundamental change in my own universe was what really captivated me. Never again would I be driving to work—or anywhere—in boy clothes, a realization that both thrilled and slightly alarmed me throughout my commute in. I savored my first elevator ride as Chloe up to my office, and my unobserved entry (I came early) through the main office doors. I mused with some relief that there would be no more furtive changes of attire in my car parked in the third basement. The time for pretending had past. It was real: I was Chloe.

But what would follow?

During the day my coworkers resisted the urge to stand and stare through my open office door, but there was a very discernible uptick in the traffic of those walking by. A few of the braver ones ventured in with words of encouragement, positive comments about my pale green skirt and white blouse, or questions about how they could be most supportive of me, all of which meant a great deal to me. The day flew by, as did the days that followed. It was quite clear to me who among my coworkers was supportive and who was disapproving, but there were also many who simply averted their eyes or otherwise gave me a wide berth. I'm sure that for many persons my transition held no interest whatsoever. Being at meetings was the hardest; I remember one young professional who dressed elegantly and wore her makeup with great care. She clearly wasn't having it, and every sour look my way made it evident that she found my presence unwelcome and offensive. I once tried to break the ice with her by asking how she applied her eyeliner so beautifully. She shrugged me off, with no intention of answering me.

Others, however, were far more gracious. Few people in my work environment felt comfortable (or interested) enough to ask any specific questions about my transition or the reasons that had given rise to it. It was a reality that I would come to experience nearly everywhere—people didn't want to know, or they seemed too shy to ask any questions. In some cases, they felt entitled to ask very inappropriate questions, mostly about surgeries. The buzz all died down after just a couple of weeks, although people continued to struggle with the pronouns. I took an interest in observing how varied the time was for people to adjust. The men in the office generally took the most time, but there were exceptions.

One significant change happened my third day on the job as Chloe. My immediate supervisor, who was the brother of the woman who is president and co-owner of the firm, summoned me into his office. I had never felt comfortable there, as the artwork of female nudes on the wall were neither artistic nor appropriate for an office environment. Bad aesthetic tastes aside, he'd done little in my time there to convince me that he had the competence or leadership skills to hold down the job that he'd been given. Still, he was the president's brother, and no one asked for my opinion regarding his competence. His gray and chrome sprawling executive corner office was furnished with two large black vinyl couches; the lights in that part of the room were always too low. He invited me to sit on a couch positioned just under one of the erotic paintings and calmly, but with some degree of exasperation, informed me that due to my "choice" it was obvious that the firm could no longer allow me to meet with any of the clients that I had normally and routinely met with. "After all," he said with a look that presumed that I ought to have internalized my shame by now, I "would be an embarrassment" to the firm. He indicated the door with a sweep of his hand; there was to be no discussion. That was it, the meeting was over.

I saw very little of management in the few months that followed, but having no access to clients made it progressively more challenging to generate revenue for the portfolio of professional services for which I was responsible. In retrospect, I shouldn't have been surprised when I was again summoned to my supervisor's corner office to be told that I was being terminated because I had failed to generate sufficient revenue. I was given a thick and imposing sheaf of legal papers to sign; these were release forms that held the firm free from any legal liability associated with my dismissal. It was explained to me that any failure on my part to sign these papers would mean that I would forfeit the modest severance pay being offered. Overwhelmed at the prospects of losing my regular income and the daunting challenge of finding new work, I signed. That was a significant mistake; under the laws of the District of Columbia they were in a weak position and should have been held accountable for their illegal actions. Fortunately for them the one-year statute of limitations expired before I was feeling sufficiently empowered to explore my legal options.

The day before I left that firm, the president invited me to her office. I'd never been in her office before; she largely remained aloof from non-executive staff and was only seen at some of the larger meetings. As I entered her beautifully furnished and elegantly appointed office, I noticed a delicate china plate of cookies and a pot of Chinese tea. The president was charming, gracious, and warm. She acknowledged with considerable candor how poorly the firm had understood and handled my transition, and how much she had learned from my poise and professionalism throughout that period. There were many smiles and kind words, and I was moved by her compassion and sincerity—at least, until I ran into an acquaintance on my way out. He was the corporate counsel, and he inquired if the president had achieved her goal to convince me not to pursue any legal recourse against the firm for wrongful dismissal! I was too embarrassed to acknowledge how brittle I felt emotionally, how she'd played me like a fiddle, and how deeply manipulated I felt from this abrupt awareness of her feigned graciousness. Damn, I hadn't even taken a cookie.

Just leaving was enough.

SEPARATION, DIVORCE, AND THEN?

Our kitchen in our University Park, Maryland home was small and woefully outdated. We struggled each day to make it function; the old wooden cupboard doors were falling apart, the countertops were chipped and unsightly, and the island counter that projected into the middle of the room was much more of an obstacle than a convenience. Two adults in that kitchen were a crowd, but it had never felt so cramped as the day when I told Christine about my diagnosis of gender dysphoria.[3]

She wasn't completely surprised. We'd lived together for fourteen years at that point, and she'd known or intuited so much of the struggle I'd been having with reconciling my masculinity with my sense of who I was. Still, we shared a bed and a marriage, and the reality of having a husband who was now deemed by an expert to be transgender was more than she could take in all at once. Drawing upon remarkable reserves of caring and understanding, her only response was: "Well . . . that makes sense."

No one person has ever known me better than Christine, and we'd already been through many struggles together in our efforts to keep our marriage grounded on intimacy, love, and respect. Given the ferocity of

---

3. *"Gender dysphoria"* is the scientific term used to describe a condition where a person experiences discomfort or distress because there's a mismatch between their biological sex and gender identity.

the dark demons we were up against, it wasn't really a surprise that in many respects we'd failed. Still, we were nowhere near thinking of our marriage as over. That tense conversation in that small kitchen, however, ended with a question that sowed the seeds of an eventual divorce: "You're not ever going to become a woman, are you?"

That was too big of a thought for me to have a ready answer for. I wasn't yet convinced that such an outcome was desirable, inevitable, or even possible. My journey up to that point had been much more about the spiritual, emotional, and mental struggle for my own identity; I'd given almost no thought yet to where it all was leading, much less any of the technicalities of gender-confirming surgical and hormonal procedures. *Becoming a woman?* I assured Christine that wasn't very likely, but as soon as I'd said the words I knew them to be problematic. What else would a diagnosis of being transgender portend? Was I destined to no longer be a man, a husband, a father? Was I instead to try to compartmentalize my life into two simultaneous personal identities, male and female, and hold that together somehow? Or was I condemned to crafting some kind of life between two genders, as some very brave people do? I just didn't know.

In time it became evident that my life had to change, and not in a small way. Around the woman and two children whom I loved most in this world I could no longer pretend to be a person I wasn't; the energy and will to sustain that complex myth were irretrievably gone. I had no guidebook for how to reprogram my life, or how to assume new roles that reflected a true expression of my identity. Those answers were within me, once I knew how to access them—I surprised myself when I found that no one had to teach me to be a woman. I also knew without doubt that I could not eradicate all that I had been; I must seek ways to carry forward the love that had defined the best elements of the old roles, even if those roles no longer fit.

I was aware quite early on that fatherhood would be the hardest part of Stephen to leave behind, simply because there wasn't any way to convey to my two young children in appropriate language the complicated and compelling reasons for my transition, and where it would leave our relationship. As my femininity found its place in the sunshine and began to blossom, the very notion of being a father seemed progressively more remote, and unassailably masculine. Perhaps I simply honored that critically important male role too much to believe that an emerging woman could justify retaining that title. Of course I was still a parent who cherished, protected, and wanted the very best for her two children, but a *father?* The sadness in letting the mantel of fatherhood slip from my grasp was poignant as I progressed into my wholeness as Chloe, especially when there was no socially acceptable feminine parental role for me to transition into. Christine was the mom. Who was I?

Transitioning has an inevitability to it, and the incremental progress in changing genders becomes a weighty force of its own. Once the decisions about transitioning became less about if and more about when, the children each strained to understand. They were also aware of their own burdens associated with this profound change, and of the possibility of being humiliated, harassed, or bullied by peers. Their fortitude, constancy, and resilience in those early years of my transition spoke volumes of their love for me, in some ways obviating any need for me to communicate a more mature understanding of the complexity of having a transgender parent. Sadly, that respite from an awkward reality wasn't entirely sustainable.

Today, many years later, I continue to struggle to define and fill a role as a successful parent. There are no scripts at the ready for a transgender mom, and no socially acceptable labels that my children are able to use to place me comfortably in their respective universes. For my son Ian, the issue is less pressing; he's completed his university years and his focus is on his future, his girlfriend Becca, and his current Peace Corps Volunteer service in Benin. He seems quite able to accept me without a label—to the degree that any message of acceptance must be communicated—and our relationship probably remains as close as any between a sixty-six-year-old parent and a not-terribly-communicative twenty-two-year-old son probably can be. I have no doubts that he has come to some inner point of reconciliation with me in his life, and that we are moving forward together in a strongly positive way even if we don't verbalize this. His wide smile and ready laugh tells me what I need to know, as does our mutual if eclectic love for classic rock 'n roll interspersed with country and western music. (I don't think I will persuade him to also adopt my love of classical music.) The few road trips we still take together on family outings are always close, always enjoyable, as Ian and I find so many common threads and common songs. He and I—and Audrey too—all share a common characteristic: we remember lyrics to hundreds of songs. Singing together makes a car journey fly by, even if it is Kenny Rogers and The First Edition's: "Just Dropped In (To See What Condition My Condition Is In)." Ian's emerging interest in a career in international development, starting with his upcoming tour of service in the Peace Corps, also provides ample territory for bonding. There is no discernible sense of hostility, no unresolved anger, no darkness within ready to poison our relationship. Ian has transitioned in his own way, and his easy love and acceptance of me is priceless.

For my seventeen-year-old daughter Audrey, creating a new parenting role remains a work in progress, but with good momentum. With no small degree of courage, in late 2015 she found the words to let me know that she was unwilling to countenance two women in her life in the traditional "mother" role, and that she had but one "home" and that home was with her biological mom. The child-sharing agreement that Christine and I forged so painfully over protracted mediation leading up to our divorce suddenly became irrelevant, leaving me adrift in a painfully empty, silent, lonely, and awkward space—physically and emotionally—outside the mother-father binary. Alone in my apartment, or when I showed up as a sporadic visitor at her "home" (i.e., at her biological mother's), my gifts as a parent did not feel particularly useful or welcomed. At that point she was but fifteen, and my presence in her life was only acceptable on her terms. That sort of arrangement is hardly unheard of among daughters of her age, but it isn't ideal for the reciprocity, affection, and discipline that a healthy parent-daughter relationship needs to flourish. Those terms just didn't work; one friend told me that in such circumstances many divorced dads simply walk away while the moms wait it all out. Curiously, my extended bout of unemployment meant that I finally needed to relinquish my small apartment and place my belongings into storage. My money was nearly gone, and Christine was kind enough to offer to sublet to me a small room in her house. It took some adjustments, but the added benefit of being back in Audrey's life on a daily basis has been the very best part of that arrangement. She and I are growing closer, and while I may not be able to claim a quasi-mom role by title, she is my daughter and we are making it work. We love each other very much.

Christine and I are no longer married, but we remain firm and committed friends. She was caring and gracious in responding to my unemployment-related financial misfortunes, inviting me to once again live with her (as a tenant) under one roof—but now it is her roof. We are making it work as a living arrangement, perhaps only as an interim measure, yet the fact that it is working quite well stands as one of life's more unexpected surprises. Back in the early stages of my transition I hadn't been thinking even remotely about divorce, and well into the many physical, emotional, and legal changes that took place I still clung to a belief that we'd find some way to make our marriage work. After all, we knew of several same-sex couples. We also knew other couples who remained married despite one partner's transition. As for assuming an identity as a same-sex married couple, Christine identifies wholly as a heterosexual woman and in time I would surprise myself by finding my own way to a similar conclusion about my own orientation, albeit with some room for bisexual possibilities. A same-sex couple comprised of two women who are both predominantly heterosexual would make for an odd marriage indeed. Yet I was so focused on marriage and how society would judge us as a married couple that I never stopped to consider that the option of two committed, caring friends sharing a house offered another way forward—and I am given to a self-effacing grimace even now as I think back to how little store I had placed in the potential of friendship to open a door to a workable, enjoyable future.

Christine's own transition, driven entirely and involuntarily by mine, was wrenching. Soon after my diagnosis she met on her own with my transgender specialist counselor Martha, and while I've never asked her the details of that meeting my guess is that Martha used that encounter to help Christine understand the clinical dynamics of being transgender and what would be likely to ensue as time progressed. Christine is herself a trained social worker, public health expert, and is now a PhD student, so her understanding of such challenges was almost certainly far better than that of most spouses who receive such alarming news. Still, the reality of losing her husband never became easier. She and I benefitted greatly from having a support group of Quakers who were as committed to her welfare and the welfare of our children as they were to me, but Christine was uniquely victimized by having to watch, powerlessly and without any control, as each change took place. My first time walking downstairs as Chloe remains an inescapable memory; I was a self-focused picture of joy and anxiety, dressed completely *en femme* and wearing a wig. As I descended into the living room where she sat watching me, I was so eager for her affirmation that the reality of her profound distress stunned—and shamed—me. She had no words to offer me; later she admitted that seeing me come into that room had been like seeing a ghost. I've never quite understood what that meant, but to this day I'm left with the poignant recollection of the painfully quizzical look that passed momentarily on her face and of my own inadequate understanding of the depth and intensity of her bewilderment. Good God—I had asked her if I looked good! It's beyond my competence now to take the measure of how insensitive I'd been at that instant, but in time I did come to recognize that the small and quivering smile she gave to me then was testimony of a remarkable capacity for grace. Her smile, at such a cost to herself, had sustained me at a moment of intense vulnerability for us both. Yes, I looked fine.

Christine has fought off breast cancer twice. She's a strong, sensible, resilient, and caring woman, and not one who would ever get comfortable with a label of "victim." That isn't to say that she did not grieve her many losses, and that she wasn't at times angry, bereft, confused, insecure, or troubled. Her despair—yet resilience—at her life's challenges and future uncertainties formed a terribly tragic counterpoint to the inevitable moments of joy in my life as I moved closer each day to healing and wholeness. This experience was captured on film when Christine, my daughter, and I accepted an invitation from the Human Rights Campaign in Washington, DC, to participate in a video that was part of their "It Gets Better" campaign. That campaign was primarily targeted at lesbian, gay, bisexual, transgender, or intersex young people who were confronting a crisis in their lives as they struggled to come to terms with their gender identity or sexual orientation. By showing examples of LGBTQI persons who have moved on to full and meaningful lives, this campaign almost certainly has prevented some suicides. My then very young daughter Audrey, Christine, and I stood before the video camera at the HRC's studio and spoke briefly about our lives. Audrey was upbeat and loving. I was full of confidence and glowing with the joy of owning my identity, basking within the warmth of a loving family. Christine was brave, and spoke of her commitment to our family—but there was no disguising the anguished tears. Once this video was published on the HRC's website, there were some very incensed women who wrote scathing comments about the inescapable reality of her deep suffering juxtaposed against my insensitive joy and our daughter's fragile innocence. I now have to admit that these critics had valid points, even if they only represented a grain of truth set against a larger and much more complicated reality. Neither Christine nor I were ready to read such reviews then, and fortunately the video was never viewed widely within our circles. Perhaps we'd do a different, more grounded video if we were invited to make one now, but one thing would be the same. Our shared love as a family that was evident in that clumsy video remains unshakable at a certain level, even if my place in the "happy family portrait" now lacks clear parameters or— for me—workable labels. An outsider would be forgiven were she or he to watch such a video and place me as a quirky aunt who had come to call.

Within our family relationship, the unfolding realities of my blossoming as Chloe and of Christine's grief as a wife who was being incrementally "widowed" created irreconcilable tension, grief, guilt, and doubt. Tense moments became the norm—moments that had their origins not in specific incidents or events, but instead in the pent-up sorrow and loss that threatened to overwhelm Christine, and in my inability to make it all go away. For a long time she endured the assumptions of others that we were a lesbian couple; she knew then and now that there isn't a single thing wrong with being part of a lesbian couple—if one were a lesbian. She bravely put her own anger aside to defend our family integrity when relatives made caustic remarks or sought to take "her side," assuming that was what she wanted. Yes, she probably did want their solidarity and their love, but not in the way that it was being offered. She knew that I hadn't chosen to be transgender, and she never showed any sign of doubting my commitment to our children and to the love and friendship that she and I still shared. Taking sides and making me the enemy would have been easy, and many lesser persons filling the role of spouse or significant other have succumbed to that script, but not Christine. To her immense credit, Christine fought her way to her own sense of agency and control, casting aside the victimhood that many caring persons wanted to bestow upon her, while clinging to a conviction that my transition was necessary and life-giving. Her current doctoral studies in social work are leading her down a new career path: to work as a researcher on the very understudied plight of spouses and children of transgender persons in America.

She is a remarkable woman.

As difficult as it was to explain my transition to my wife and my children, it remained nearly as daunting to explain the necessity of a gender transition to those close to our small family. People who cared about both of us could also see Christine's pain and her emptiness as her husband no longer wore his former clothes, as Chloe unapologetically took Stephen's place. They would question first whether this transition was really necessary at all, and failing that, whether it could not be slowed down significantly or compartmentalized in some way. Some would cite stories they'd heard of cross-dressing spouses who renegotiated their marriages to allow for this form of gender expression *discreetly* without jeopardizing their marriages. The intentions of such caring friends and associates were laudable, but the genie was not to be put back into the bottle. As Chloe, I was gaining more fullness and authenticity with each passing day; you might as well tell the butterfly emerging from the chrysalis to stay inside, or to emerge more slowly. Chloe, like the butterfly, was fighting for her life—my life. At that stage the outcome was by no means clear or certain.

As the HRC video campaign asserted, it does get better—but it can be a fraught journey to get there. Over time we've mostly found our way, but not without many sacrifices, much pain, and awkwardness. Christine and I entered into mediation, and through that emotionally draining but well-facilitated process we arrived at a separation agreement and then ultimately a divorce. She and I continue to rediscover the essential reasons that drew us together first as friends, while each recognizing that our lives have moved progressively apart, with occasional (and often protracted) periods of congenial collaboration and closeness. For a year we jointly leased a house with separate bedrooms, giving us some time to each get our bearings. Then we moved to separate accommodations only 300 yards apart on the same street, making it easy for our daughter to move from house to house. Then Christine and Audrey moved to a townhouse three miles away. And then, as fate would have it, I moved back in with Christine as a tenant, albeit as a temporary measure while I wait for my ship to come in—to find a job—and regain my financial footing.

In some very important ways we both know that the worst days of our struggle are behind us, but that the journey still remains a hard one. Perhaps Christine and I now have much more freedom, making it possible for each of us to find our separate ways to a friendship and a co-parenting relationship that benefits all four of us, and one that we can sustain for years to come. Yet even as I now sit alone in my small room upstairs in her house, that's not a sure thing. We both have to continue to work on this, and where we will find ourselves in the years to come remains a mystery.

DESTINATION: SISTERHOOD

Long before my transition journey commenced, I'd been on a quest for the sisterhood. As a younger person I took only small comfort in knowing that many men and boys have wonderful and entirely platonic relationships with women and girls. The evidence was abundant; sharing daily lived realities between men, women, and genderqueer persons does provide a basis for building friendships that are strong, durable, and meaningful. I had spent much of my life exploiting that edge, feeling so tightly drawn to girls and women, yet knowing how complicated it was while embodied as a boy or man to draw close without fear of having my intentions misinterpreted. Throughout my high school years in Potsdam, I tried on a regular basis to forge and sustain such friendships with varying success. Chemistry complicates such relationships, and testosterone-induced turbulence is not to be underestimated despite the most asexual of intentions. Still, I did cultivate close friendships with a few high school girls, frequently joining them on prolonged evening telephone calls in which everything and nothing was discussed, fervently. My telephonic network in those pre-texting days was exclusively girls, except for me. I never cared, but some of my female friends' mothers were quite unsettled by my participation, attributing it to some devious or "creepy" intention on my part to weasel my way into their trust and hence to earn their affections and become a traditional boyfriend. I wasn't remotely so strategic; I just liked the company of girls.

Throughout my life that immovable barrier between the sexes has always been apparent to me, as the Chloe buried within me sought sisterhood in a world that constrained such relationships. I lived with that tension, and sometimes managed to convert it into a dynamic and energizing force within friendly relationships with women. Still, I always balked at the barrier. My most important relationship with any woman, with the woman who later became my wife and the mother of my two children, began with a deep and entirely platonic friendship. Christine was a young woman of insight, warmth, and sensitivity far beyond her years, who shared my penchant for writing in the margins of books, talking about spirituality and feminism, and of being fascinated by a world full of adventures and discoveries. We'd meet regularly over tea or coffee at a now-demolished French café in the Adams Morgan district of Washington, feeling sophisticated and terribly cosmopolitan as we nursed our hot mugs at the small round tables and talked for hours while the busy citizens of Washington streamed by the large plate-glass windows. We could have been easily distracted by the people passing by, resplendent in their Central American bright colors, and by the jaunty loud Spanish music outside in this most Hispanic of Washington's neighborhoods, but our eyes and ears were only for each other. It took hours, and much tea and coffee, to build that durable friendship, yet in time that friendship would become a love and a deep, abiding affection.

While never attaining the level of the profound friendship and ultimately the transcendent (if ultimately platonic) intimacy that characterizes my ongoing relationship with Christine, other women also seemed to see and respond to the Chloe nature within me. I'd often spend evenings, lunches, and long walks with such women, and be shaped and sustained by their care and natural femininity. Many of these friendly encounters were linked to specific moments in my life; these women in time moved on or became in one way or another inaccessible, or remained "friendly" but no longer close. One of them, a bisexual woman from Austin, Texas (and the first out bisexual I had ever known), established an easy (and entirely platonic) rapport with me in the early 1990s that felt wonderfully woman-to-woman as we would talk over a bottle of cheap wine late into the night in her sparsely furnished Capitol Hill apartment. I have tried to locate her over the years, but have never succeeded. In retrospect, I have little doubt that she perceived Chloe within me long before I fully came to appreciate this reality myself, but it would be wonderful to talk it all through with her now.

Another exceptional person among the "other women" was Karen Vondy, a university classmate of my former girlfriend Gillian—both Brits. Karen was very special, with a generous warmth and prodigious intellect embodied in a beautiful woman of compassion, empathy, and deep insights. Even after she married a very handsome (and very humorous) Irish-Australian lawyer named Tony and then gave birth to their two children, she and I stayed close friends. In time Christine also created her own special friendship with her and her husband. When I came out, Karen was one of the few friends who got the balance right by asking me the important accountability questions about what would be the impact on Christine and the children, instead of simply being gushy with supportive enthusiasm. Karen knew how to listen; it took very little time to communicate to her the reasons for my transition, and my continuing deep care for and commitment to my family. She quickly came to support me with a degree of warmth and acceptance that few were able to match. When she passed away from breast cancer, I felt her loss acutely, and in many ways I still grieve her loss. Friends like Karen are rare, and I cherish the time that I had her friendship in my life.

Given the international character of my life and career, my friends are widely dispersed geographically. Friends who are separated by vast distances remain as close as email and Facebook can sustain. Sarah, a remarkable and courageous Ugandan lawyer and feminist, who helped me through a period of deep crisis in my pre-transition life, was one such friend. Sarah almost uniquely perceived—and honored—the feminine me that was struggling like never before in my life to break free, and she has gone on to become a strong and effective ally of transgender people like me in her own country. An example of an empowered confident woman, Sarah offered nonjudgmental support as I first looked into the mirror of womanhood. Her friendship opened my eyes and my spirit to the Chloe who was staring back at me from that mirror. Still other women have become fast friends after my transition even if we see each other only periodically; I think in particular of my dear friends Veronika and Jody, who each bring to our respective friendships deep empathy and unself-conscious affection.

Even with the allure and comfort of these remarkable women within the sisterhood to support me, there's nothing smooth about the gender transition experience. The ups are often exhilarating, validating, and revelatory, but the downs can be jolting and harsh, filled with anxieties, societal and family pressures, and a poignant sense of vulnerability. During one of the more desolate down periods I spoke on the phone with my sister Barb, who lives with her husband in Seattle. Her support at that critical juncture was instrumental in helping me get through it all, and she's remained a trusted and understanding friend. May 28, 2008, was a particularly down day, but it was my good fortune to receive an email from Barb. I was feeling drained from perceiving myself (whether correctly or not) as someone whose presence made my wife deeply uncomfortable and embarrassed, and whose transition threatened the security, order, innocence, and joy of my children's lives. I dreaded the prospect of being pathetic—a man in a dress—which is really to say the prospect of committing all of my dignity, identity, hopes, career and fatherhood to what I thought may be an impossible and perhaps ludicrous dream—joining the sisterhood. Barb's short message turned that mood around promptly when she wrote:

> *You are at such a hard part of this whole transition, and my heart just goes out to you. Please, please know that there are so many wonderful parts of being a woman, and part of the sisterhood of women, and you ARE going to be a part of that sisterhood soon.*

Battling these insecurities and mood swings was typical of the awkward early stages of my journey from male to female embodiment, when I didn't yet know how to connect with what it felt like to be a woman. I wasn't quite ready to reach inside to where that answer simply lay waiting, and instead sought my validation from some notional "community of women," or sisterhood. I once shared with Barb how much my journey at that point felt akin to my many earlier experiences as a rock climber. My transition journey was the very steep cliff in front of me, and I was using my best judgment to find a viable route up that cliff face. Like nearly all cliffs, the first few feet up are always okay, because I know that I can always hop down without injury. But that option quickly evaporates as I climb higher on the face, and I get to the point where the climb demands total concentration and total commitment. The possibility of falling is tangibly real, and although the protection (clamps, wedges, and devices that climbers jam into the cracks to hold their safety ropes) offers some security from a fatal fall, a fall will still hurt, and the cliff remains to be climbed. I only have so much energy, but will it be enough? Perhaps the path that I have chosen up the rock is a dead end and gets to an unclimbable point—then what? At least with a great deal of rock climbing experience, as I had, I knew what to do and what my strengths were. There's all that adrenaline too. Standing on tiny ledges of rock hundreds of feet off the ground does tend to concentrate the mind on the task ahead. But that's where the analogy came apart: while I was an accomplished rock climber, I didn't know what I was doing in this transition. There was no practice, no class, and no mentor. It all had to be learned on the journey, with only a few bits and pieces that I could glean from books like Jenny Boylan's *She's Not There*, or the pioneering 1974 book *Conundrum* by Jan Morris, and similar sources online and off. Gender transitions don't generate as much adrenalin as rock climbing either, except from fear of being "read" as a man. The top of the gender-transition cliff often feels impossibly high. Finally, there's a point where it is obvious that there isn't even a safety rope or any type of protection. Unless I could find my way to a conviction in the possibility of success in this journey for an ordinary transgender person like me, and not just for the likes of famous transgender women like Jenny Boylan or Jan Morris, how would I find the strength and energy to reach the top of that perilous cliff? Would there be any actual sense of arrival, or confirmation that being a transgender woman offered a viable, meaningful life for me? More alarming still was my awareness of having already passed the divide—the no-turning-back point when climbing down that steep cliff would have been far harder than continuing to climb up.

One of my more persistent anxieties at that time had to do with the prospect of inadvertently "third-gendering" myself, and finding myself stuck halfway in my transition in a category that I didn't aspire to. While some persons are comfortable outside the gender binary, my own sense of authenticity has been and remains emphatically at the female end of the spectrum. But the question remained open: Would women receive me as one of them, and were their embraces needed to validate me? Could I be truly self-ish without their validation? And what about men? In retrospect, it's perhaps curious how little thought I gave then to my departure from the world of men. Perhaps because I simply assumed (incorrectly, it transpires) that I would transition into a lesbian, I didn't even wonder whether men would accept me as a woman. That question of male acceptance, or even male interest in me as a sexual and/or romantic partner, has come back to haunt me now. Men—at least men anywhere close to my age—all seem totally unable to wrap their minds around the fact that Chloe is a woman. Period. And while it's a common (and often rudely ridiculed) complaint among single cisgender women my age that finding a compatible and attractive single man is nearly an impossibility, I have come to learn that being in a similar status while also being transgender is akin to having a bad case of leprosy. Men—as far as my survey has taken me— can't deal with even the idea of intimacy and romance with women like me. That's an awkward and ultimately self-annihilating form of survey, and I have curbed that part of my journey for now. Men will just have to make do without me. Still, at that early time of my transition when I was so intent on my own journey, what men thought about me mattered little so long as they did not think I was one of them. I certainly did not look to men to offer support.

That's not to say that I did not seek out support. I did; I pushed myself to try a transgender support group. Simply getting to that decision, and then implementing that decision, took an enormous amount of psychic energy as I somehow rallied the courage to attend. It's a group called the Metro Area Gender Identity Connection (MAGIC for short) and the drive there was long. It was at the earliest stages of my transition and I therefore arrived still entirely presenting in boy mode, and found a gathering of around fifteen individuals at every stage of transition. I remember almost nothing from that first time there except the logistical difficulties of finding where, in that large church complex, the meeting was being held. Once that obstacle was overcome, I joined the assembled persons with a profound sense of wonder (and, truth be told, disquiet) as to whether this was really "my community" now, while simultaneously feeling great empathy and dismay as some who were there described heart-rending stories of rejection and humiliation. Then the facilitator of the group, Jessica, turned and gave me an intensive stare. Without even asking whether I was merely exploring or actually underway in my transition, this very well put-together transgender woman declared that I would have no trouble *passing* as a woman once I had transitioned. Her validating and matter-of-fact words astounded me as much as they delighted me, and her assessment got me through so many tough moments in the months and years to follow. I'm forever in her debt; Jessica has selflessly given so much support and time to the transgender community. No one makes a successful gender transition without support from the likes of a Jessica, and I'm sure I'm not alone in my admiration of her generosity of spirit and caring.

One of the earliest tangible steps in my transition, at the urging of my therapist Martha, was getting started on the physical logistics. Facial hair removal is an enormous undertaking, and expensive. I began with laser treatments, which probably removed thirty percent of all whiskers, but did nothing for the seventy percent that stubbornly remained. I then (often painfully) worked through a series of electrologists of widely varying skills before finally finding my way to Mona. She's a no-nonsense, salt-of-the-earth Jewish woman, steeped in her faith traditions, and wise in the ways of the world. In no time at all she became a dear friend and confidant, and I had ample opportunity to deepen that relationship. Over the many years to come my electrolysis would extend to well over 300 hours, each hour filled with sharp pain and even some tears, but Mona's calm and caring professionalism was only trumped by her complete acceptance of me as a woman. She was the first woman I had ever really engaged with woman-to-woman on so many issues, from the trifling to the sensitive, from minor chitchat to trusted confidences. In our time together her husband would pass away, I would have my surgery, she would travel to Israel, and I would become a divorcée. I would rise to amazing career heights first as an Obama administration political appointee and then a vice president of a major human rights organization, and would fall to the deep lows of extended unemployment. Mona was my rock, and a strong connection to the world of women.

The other women to whom I reached out to for support were therapists, and their time also came with costs attached. I was trying to manage my escalating transition expenses by alternating my therapy sessions between the transgender expert Martha and a less expensive local therapist whom I will refer to as Kay (not her real name). It was clear however that Kay was already well out of her depth, as she avoided transition-related discussions and kept urging me to spend time trying to heal my inner child. I told her that I didn't see much point in healing that damaged little boy until after we'd found and healed the little girl—Chloe—who hadn't just popped into my existence at age fifty-seven. She too had a past worth reaching for. Kay wanted to keep me grounded and was cautious of inflated expectations; she especially did not want me to idealize some fictitious female mystique. I explained to her that I needed something to grasp, some shade of happiness that I dared to believe in (without feeling that I was being too audacious). I knew that there were women who love to be women (and men who love to be men); what I did not know was how to find those women or even how to have that conversation about why they love their womanhood. Who shares that sort of thing, especially to someone still presenting (at least part of the time) as a man?

I soon ended the sessions with Kay, as they left me feeling vulnerable, sometimes unwisely adventurous, and often self-consciously foolish—especially while first changing into feminine garb in her office's restroom, and then reversing that process at the end of the session. Hauling my girl-clothes in two plastic bags into her office felt like being in a play, not like entering into a space where those clothes signified authenticity. It was clear to me that Kay could not be persuaded, which unsettled me but also challenged me to move stubbornly (and perhaps even a bit fiercely) past her evident skepticism. The sessions too were often marked by hurt and darkness. It wasn't just Kay; before I found Martha (who works exclusively with transgender persons and their families), attempts at therapy often reminded me of my gender dissonance—and that much of my adult life had been defined by a deep inner rejection. At least I now had the words; before I had only known that I'd been wanting so much to have the maleness taken away from me. Still, there wasn't much, if any, that was positive in my new-found clarity. I couldn't yet access any clear image of myself as a woman waiting to emerge from her long sleep. Kay could only invite me into a place of cold emptiness by directing me to talk about not being a man, and about my embarrassing history of coping techniques by which I had embraced extreme physical pain and humiliation to separate myself from that male reality. What I most needed to talk through with her was the existential reality of Chloe, and the memory and continuing experiential desolation of being Chloe while also being submerged in that messy past, ignored and lost. I yearned to come to grips with the story of an unsung hero, a resolute girl tenaciously resilient against all odds, awaiting her entrance. Kay wasn't willing or able to help me find her, revive her, or envision a happy, viable future for her . . . which of course meant Kay was not able or willing to move my sessions with her to a place where we could discuss a happy, viable future for me.

In time, however, the truth became inescapable; I only had to give myself to it and not try so hard. The sisterhood *is* all around me and within me. It has become most beautifully and deeply accessible through the annual Quakers' Women's Retreats held amidst Maryland's bleak, snowy, and frigid January winter. There I've connected to and found my place within that sisterhood in ways more complex, warm, and unexpectedly meaningful than I could have ever imagined. I've even recently found myself invited into a remarkable vocational sisterhood I never could have imagined finding.

I am Chloe, and my life as a woman is more satisfying than I ever dared to imagine. Even in less elevated or formal settings, I have found to my great joy that the sisterhood is now, it is here, and it is accessible. Women have as many flaws as men, but the sisterhood remains a common bond uniting all women at some level, whether they are willing to acknowledge this or not. It comes out of a special world view, a uniquely female way of being in and of the world and of each other. It is simultaneously embracing and thorny, and I flourish within it—thorns and all.

Being present and whole within the sisterhood has alone been worth the journey.

TRANSGRESSING "NO!"

Standing (left to right): Carol Schwenke, Barb Cartmell, George Schwenke, Janet Schwenke, Chloe Schwenke, Roger Schwenke

Seated (left to right): Ken Schwenke, Amanda Schwenke

REJECTION

How would you feel if a person you know to be otherwise rational and intelligent purposely referred to you by the wrong name and gender pronoun? They do it not just once, but again and again, in a crowd of people—a crowd which includes you. My supposition is that you'd assume that the person in question was acting very strangely indeed. If you're a transgender person in that same situation, however, the meaning would be clear. The speaker is making a public statement of rejecting your identity, smugly reassured that all those in that crowd (with the exception of you, and you clearly don't matter) will align with this critique. It's a direct put-down, a public challenge to your fundamental identity and an opportunity to shame you for your audacity. Sadly, it's anything but an uncommon experience for me and many other transgender persons.

Every transgender person knows there will be occasional slips and mistakes as people reorient themselves to you. When a transgender person crosses the gender threshold, everyone she or he knows must also come to terms with that transition. Ignoring someone's gender transition isn't an option. In many important ways, the people most closely within the sphere of that transgender person's life must examine and lay bare their own perceptions of gender identity and come to some peace with those like me who feel compelled to journey in those tangled spaces. It's not all bleak; I think back to the gutsy vitality and refreshing boldness with which many of the African-American women in my former place of work together stepped into my transition and ultimately embraced it. For others in my life, however, it was neither easy nor comfortable, and some people pushed back in ways that I still associate with sharp memories of pain, dismay, and disappointment.

Elderly people frequently have a very difficult time breaking years or even decades of habit. My mother died in 2005, just two years before I started my transition, but my father was eighty-nine when I came out to him, with Christine by my side, in his small kitchen at his extended care facility apartment in Largo, Florida. His initial struggle to comprehend what we were both sharing with him was written across his face and in the wide-open eyes with which he took us both in. At least he was familiar with the basics; his local town manager Susan Stanton (formerly Steve Stanton) had recently come out as a transgender woman—a courageous admission for which she had been fired amid national media attention. My father had read all about it not long before our conversation. Still, this was his son saying that she was in fact his daughter. A retired US Marine colonel, my dad had a healthy respect for those in authority, and he was somewhat comforted by my reports of the well-qualified experts ("authorities") who had been working closely with me throughout the diagnosis and initial transition processes, and by learning of the growing body of empirical reports on the veracity and impact of the transgender phenomenon. Still, he was overcome with worry, and he managed to vocalize his concern that I might be subject to violence when using the men's room. My assurances that I had been consistently using the women's room for many months left him searching for something to say next. Throughout this conversation and in the months ahead, there was never a moment when I doubted his love for us both and for our children. Yes, he went through some time of being fiercely angry at God for allowing such a thing to have happened to his son (and to him, I presume), but he was never once angry to me.

I had been under considerable pressure from my siblings to "put on the boy clothes" and just pretend, to spare the dear old colonel the anguish of having to leap this chasm of understanding. I sat a long time with that request, but I just couldn't accede. My relationship with my dad was one of the most important relationships of my life. Carrying that relationship forward based upon an existential lie was no way to honor his love, and it would have been beyond my own emotional strength and my commitment to integrity to have pursued such a ruse. Fortunately, the staff at his extended care facility were very supportive of me, and did all that they could to help my father find his own peace with having a new daughter. I doubt it was easy for him. He frequently lapsed into the old name and pronouns, especially when speaking with me on the telephone before I had mastered moving my voice into a feminine register, but he was consistently and graciously receptive to being steered back to grammatical correctness, often with a warm chuckle at his mistake. My final year with him became a time of remarkable closeness, in which he shared many very personal thoughts and memories in ways that conveyed his acceptance of Chloe and his love for his children—no matter how they were packaged.

Incorrect names and pronouns are annoyances, even if significant annoyances. In time it all gets resolved, but in the middle stages of a transition it can often seem to be getting worse. I don't know a single transgender person who hasn't run into more than a few walls of outright rejection, humiliation, and hostility on this score. In many of the countries where I often work, that rejection frequently becomes violent. I count myself lucky; no one who is really close to me failed to come around in due course, nor have I been the victim of violence. Hate mail from the army of Internet trolls, yes, but never any physical violence.

Some people took their time adjusting (in some cases many years); in the interim their rejection took the form of distancing themselves from me, avoiding conversations, and generally backing away. Two of my male siblings struggled mightily with my change in identity; despite my pleas to them that we make some time to sit down together, hear each other out, and then discuss. They remained resolutely uncommunicative, and it felt inappropriately self-centered to push this conversation onto them. After several years they gradually relented and found a place of acceptance, although that specific conversation never took place. It's now clear to me that they had each found their own path to understanding (or if not understanding, at least accepting) my transition; to my delight (and relief) they have now each made room in their hearts for their new sister. To this day, when any of my siblings introduces me to others as "my sister Chloe" it feels very special indeed; I can only guess how hard their journey was to get to those words. Their love got them there; so yes—it does get better.

For others, the rejection isn't personal. They just don't get it. I've had two male acquaintances come to me, separately, to ask for a chance to discuss "all of this" over a cup of coffee or lunch. In both cases I was happy to oblige, with the only caveat being that they set aside adequate time. The resulting conversations were caring, frank, and comprehensive, and they achieved the goal of creating a base of understanding. In both cases, the resulting friendships have built upon that base to positive effect.

Among the hardest rejections are the silent ones; people who reject you and refuse to discuss this with you. They often decide not to even acknowledge their misgivings or uncertainties. Essentially, these people just wrote me off. I was too "complicated" for them to put in the reflective work needed to understand my situation, and they weren't able to simply trust that it was okay for me to be a transgender woman (or to be a woman at all). They assumed a permanent stance of rejection and dismissal.

There were of course numerous official rejections, or at least procrastinations. The IRS, credit card companies, banks, voter registration offices, the Social Security Administration, utilities and other service providers, doctors and dentists, mortgage bankers and title companies, life insurance companies, airline frequent-flier programs, car and home insurance providers, other corporate connections, and many others sometimes only are willing to make these changes in their records after persistent cajoling. Mailing lists continue sending their notices, solicitations, and junk mail to the old name, and the only solution I ever found was to wait until I moved my residence. Even then some "Stephen" mail would follow me (and still does), in which case the only effective tactic available to me has been to call up their mailing department and feign to be the widow of the late Stephen Schwenke, requesting that they show the decency to stop sending their materials to my late husband. That almost always works.

Where American corporations, service providers, and officialdom were slow moving or cranky, Turkish bureaucracy was shamelessly abusive. In October 2008 I traveled to Izmir, Turkey to run a training seminar on ethical leadership, funded by the British government. I was already living full-time as Chloe and had legally changed my name, but hadn't yet undergone gender-confirming surgery. Under the federal rules at that time I was unable to have my gender marker changed on my passport until after surgery; my passport therefore announced me to the world as Chloe Schwenke, but the gender marker remained "M." Just to cover my bases, Martha had provided me with a "To Whom It May Concern" letter on her letterhead paper that explained among other things that "Chloe must present herself in female attire as part of her therapeutic regime" and further asserted that I "should be accorded all the rights of being female." Given Turkey's appalling record of discrimination against women,

I knew from the outset that such rights were questionable at best, but I was entirely unprepared for what would actually take place, starting with the Transportation Security Administration (TSA) officers at nearby Dulles International Airport in Virginia. In the middle of the usual long line of waiting passengers, I gestured to a TSA officer to come over, and I showed her my letter and asked if I needed to do anything in order to avoid a delay at the scanner machine. She had no idea, passed my letter to another TSA officer, who in turn passed it to the supervisory TSA officer on duty—all the while the line shuffled forward to the waiting scanners. He pulled me out of the line, read and reread the letter, and after some delay and considerable head-scratching, my therapist's letter worked. He shrugged, led me back into the line, and without further fuss I boarded my plane. During the lengthy flight, I had many opportunities to worry about what reception lay ahead. My hope was that the Turkish immigration officials would only look at the name on my passport and at me, a convincingly feminine person. It didn't quite work out that way; bleary-eyed after the long flight, I probably wasn't looking my feminine best, so perhaps the Turkish immigration officer had more reason to stare at my passport than at me. Almost immediately, he asked me about the "M" on my passport.

The Turkish immigration official spoke the most rudimentary English, and my Turkish language skills don't exist. My attempts at explaining the transgender transition process, and my beautifully typed and signed letter of explanation from my therapist were both a complete waste of time. He kept my passport and waved me over to stand aside and wait, where I stood for over an hour until the lobby was empty of passengers. He never looked up at me at all, just left me to stand and wait. Then that immigration officer finally did look up, fixing me with a hard and sustained stare that was openly hostile, before he turned away to beckon to the other five (all male) immigration officers on duty. They were happy for the distraction; they'd all been standing about with nothing to do in the lull between plane arrivals. Not one of them had paid me any attention at all, but that suddenly changed as the original officer waved my passport around to summon them all to encircle me. There they took turns examining my passport, amid loud guffaws and exclamations in Turkish—but they never looked me in the eyes. Instead I watched, powerless and frightened, as their eyes traveled up and down my body as if I were a suspicious—or at least curious—inanimate object. Next, each had to take his turn examining my passport, with each passing his own judgment on the "M" in my passport. Each of them dramatized this process by pointing at the "M," then at me, then at my passport, then at me, then passing my passport on to their next colleague. Their mood was initially jovial, but the mirth changed very quickly to scathing judgments in halting English about the deterioration of masculinity in America, and how I ought to feel ashamed to disguise myself as a woman (clearly a step in the wrong direction, in their worldview). They accompanied these acerbic comments with further loud guffaws and taunts in Turkish. They did not touch me, but in their encirclement they were uncomfortably close. It all felt like it went on for a very long time; obviously making humiliating comments in Turkish directed at or about me was proving to be a great source of amusement while they waited for the next planeload of passengers to come through. When those passengers finally arrived, I was again told to wait, and another hour went by. In the end I was at the airport until the next shift of immigration officers (again, all male) came on duty, so that the former shift could "introduce" me to them, and the whole process of encirclement, taunts and caustic comments was resumed, but with new participants. It went just like before, although this time I was in tears, and I was so exhausted. Before I was finally waved through, I had been at the airport for more than four hours, and it seemed to take that long again before I regained my composure and overcame my tears. In the next few days, I had the good sense to report all of this to the American Consulate and found the staff to be supportive, caring, and empathetic. I don't know what, if anything, they actually did about this incident, but my subsequent departure at the airport went without incident. I've not been back to Izmir, although I have been to Istanbul and Ankara, securely brandishing my new "F" passport.

It wasn't just Turkish officialdom that stood in my way to full self-ishness. In September of 2009, getting the gender marker changed on my driver's license in my own East Coast, liberal state of Maryland proved to be a monumental ordeal as well. Even after having undergone gender-confirming surgery by that time, and with appropriate documentation to that effect from my surgeon and my gynecologist, the two Motor Vehicle Administration (MVA) offices that I went to both adamantly refused to make the change. In the second attempt, at the MVA office in Gaithersburg, the manager was called up to where I waited at the information booth in the main lobby. Amidst a large crowd of people waiting in line he berated me in a loud and smug voice: "I don't care how you may have modified your private parts, you're always going to be a man on that license." The ensuing hush in that large room was intimidating, but he clearly relished the spotlight. Every eye was on us, as he demonstrated with his body language and his words how unimpressed he was that my passport showed me as female. He also made it clear—again very loudly in that now silent room—how he had no interest in any of the other documentation that attested to the fact that I was indeed now anatomically fully female. After he held up each of these letters and documents and waved them about contemptuously, playing to the crowd, I was flushed with embarrassment. My only recourse was to grab back my documents and leave, feeling every eye upon me and hearing the rising tide of comments, guffaws, and discussion behind me. Fortunately, I later had the good sense (and stubbornness) to pursue matters through many formal letters to the MVA's case review manager, and ultimately to the office of Governor Martin O'Malley. With the governor's direct intervention, I finally won my "F" from the MVA, and fortunately the process is now much easier for those who have followed me in making this request. Hopefully that abusive manager has retired; I never heard what became of him.

STEREOTYPES

I can't even recall the name of the event, since such events are fairly commonplace and frequent in Washington, DC. There we all were—a gathering of transgender women from around the United States. It was midway in my own transition, probably around 2010, and both Mara Keisling and Amanda Simpson gave short speeches. Mara is indomitable, smart, bitingly funny, and exudes confidence; she and her small staff have done so much good work on behalf of American transgender persons through her courageous leadership and remarkable energy at the helm of the National Center for Transgender Equality (NCTE) in Washington—an organization that she founded.[4] Amanda was the first transgender woman political appointee in the Obama administration, and she was working at that time for the Department of Commerce. She later transferred over to the Pentagon, where she continued her competent and highly regarded service until the end of the Obama era; in doing so, she managed to shatter all manner of wicked stereotypes. I don't remember if Dylan Orr, a transgender man who was the very first transgender political appointee (Department of Labor), was present, but I wouldn't have been surprised.

---

4. I had the good fortune of doing a six-week consulting gig at NCTE early in 2017, providing legislative outreach and lobbying to Congress as the organization pivoted to address the many challenges inherent in the Trump presidency and the Republican lock on Congress. My admiration for Mara, and the staff at the NCTE, only grew.

Dylan is a stalwart champion of transgender rights in the United States. After Mara's and Amanda's excellent speeches, the mood in the room was buoyant.

Still, I recall feeling very awkward and ill at ease. I had impulsively sat at a table of four transgender women all in their fifties or sixties, and all from Midwest states. They were each large of stature, with somewhat gravelly voices, and faces that remained stubbornly masculine. I knew right away that each of their lives must be so challenging; our society is ruthlessly unforgiving to transgender women who struggle to "pass." Yet there they were, uplifted by each other's presence, and thrilled to be at that gathering. Their delight to be at that table was manifest in their broad smiles, and they were very cordial to me in that reliable Midwestern way. Wonderful women, each and every one of them; I do hope that I reciprocated in kind.

Despite their congeniality, I'm acutely embarrassed now to confess that as soon as I sat down at their table I wished I could've found somewhere else to sit. I wanted so deeply not to be *them*, and not to be viewed by others outside the transgender community in the same way. Certainly I didn't want to be the embodiment of one of the worst transgender stereotypes: the man in a dress. The whole luncheon was colored by my realization that being among transgender women was not where I wanted to be, but that I was well past the point of no return. I simply wanted to be Chloe, a woman, and not Chloe, a transgender woman.

Nothing excuses the meanness of my mindset that day, but with the distance of time and now being so settled in my identity as Chloe I can forgive myself a little. I was frightened, and at that vulnerable stage of my own transition I was very worried about my future. Safety and security are the most fundamental needs of any person in any situation, and at that time and in that place I felt neither. I've long since moved on, and now am honored and delighted to find my place among any transgender persons anywhere. We all share so much, even if each of us has a unique story. As my friend Dylan—a trans man—is fond of saying, "When you've heard one transgender person's story, you've heard one transgender person's story!" That's largely true, but we all face many of the same obstacles—pernicious stereotypes rooted in ignorance chief among them. We face them every day in the media, in casual conversations, in passing comments, and in decisions made that directly affect our future prospects. I've written often to National Public Radio, the Washington Post, and other respected media outlets to express concern about "humor" or stories that exploit or distort the plight of transgender persons. I push back about their misinformation that confounds our efforts to overcome ignorance about who we are, or about missed opportunities (mostly when they are discussing issues of sexual orientation such as same-sex marriage) to offer a small comment in passing that would let readers or listeners know that the "T" (for transgender people) exists, that we are here, and that our stories are primarily about gender identity and not to be conflated with sexual orientation. As far as the mainstream media goes, we are all simply "gay," which makes invisible the lives and challenges of many transgender people. Personally, I have become something of a bore (or what we once called a "broken record") speaking out indignantly on this topic, yet my experience is that I find myself and the transgender community labeled as "gay" so often. I also bristle when people use "LGBTQI" to discuss exclusively gay and lesbian issues. It's almost certainly a losing battle—the media have us firmly under the gay tent, but calling all transgender people "gay" obscures what it is like to be us—transgender.

All marginalized persons confront stereotypes. It's what the majority do to "others," and perhaps it's hardwired into human nature. Many of these stereotypes do great damage to their targets, limiting our chances of being accepted as part of the recognized diversity of the human condition. Stereotypes of the awkward "man in a dress" cast us as powerless victims of our own mental instabilities, the butt of jokes and sniggers, people who are by definition exemplars of humiliation, stigma, and otherness. It's why I cannot rewatch that otherwise funny old Woody Allen film *Everything You Wanted to Know about Sex*. That film has one vignette in which the actor Lou Jacobi is cast as a middle-class Jewish man who feels compelled to cross-dress. Seeing this man's shame as he is discovered dressed in drag elicited boisterous laughs in the movie theater, but not from me, even way back in 1972 when the film was released. Cross-dressing isn't necessarily indicative of being transgender, but even a cross-dresser who doesn't identify as transgender is not deserving of ridicule and belittlement. That film came out over forty years ago, but still to this day the prospect of an awkward transgender person or unpersuasive cross-dresser finds its way into comedy routines all the time. I'm now perpetually on alert watching *Saturday Night Live* (where the humor is otherwise a much-needed balm to assuage the rough edges of enduring the Trump administration), as *SNL* has twice (at least while I watched) sacrificed the dignity and humanity of transgender folk in exchange for a laugh at our expense. One *SNL* show in 2011 had a mock advertisement for estrogen therapy, ridiculing transgender women by featuring an overweight middle-aged man (with ample facial hair) dressed in women's attire. Much more recently, *SNL* host Colin Jost asserted that the reason Hillary Clinton lost her bid for the presidency was because the dating app Tinder had introduced non-binary gender classifications. Overlooked in such cheap-laugh humor is the fact that a transgender woman in a dress isn't a man at all, or that the socially imposed rigidity of the gender binary can be an insufferable straightjacket for many transgender people. Some cisgender people push back, arguing that I am being overly sensitive, but people need to learn that laughing at transgender people when they are reduced to a comical absurdity isn't okay. "It's just a joke" can dehumanize us in ways that are far from harmless; the extremely high rate of suicides and attempted suicides for transgender Americans is no laughing matter. Statistically no other American demographic comes close to that somber suicide distinction.[5]

Pernicious stereotypes are spread and sustained by the media, and American media has much to answer for this. I won't attempt to summarize the excellent and appropriately scathing review of the media that well-known transgender woman Julia Serano provided in chapter two of her marvelous book *Whipping Girl: A Transsexual Woman on Sexism and the Scapegoating of Femininity*, originally published in 2007 and updated in a second edition in 2016. Suffice it to say that most portrayals of transgender persons in print or film depict us as pathetic, mentally unstable, sex-crazed victims, or people given to deceit and to leading hapless men astray. The media largely ignores transgender men, but then the media has regularly shown a predilection for the objectification and sexualization of women, transgender or not. Even the few more credible efforts to portray transgender persons humanely such as the television series *Transparent*, or the made-for-television 2003 movie *Normal*, are fundamentally flawed by casting their respective transgender characters using actors who themselves are not transgender. Jeffrey Tambor and Richard Bull are fine and talented actors, but would we accept a Caucasian actor playing an African-American person? It makes no sense, and is a disservice to transgender persons. Okay, I'll make an exception for Eddie Redmayne who was cast as historic transwoman and artist Lili Elbe in the 2015 film, *The Danish Girl*. To date, I have yet to see a more

---

5. The 2015 US Transgender Survey by NCTE revealed that 40 percent of the nearly 28,000 transgender participants surveyed had attempted to take their own lives at some point. By comparison, only 4.6 percent of the overall US population has self-reported a suicide attempt.

moving and sensitive portrayal of our lives; it reduced me to tears with its poignant depiction of that very early attempt at a medically-assisted gender transition.

There are a few positive signs, however, even in the media. For many years, I have appreciated that Oprah brought transgender persons onto her television show and let viewers see them—us—as interesting, genuine, but refreshingly ordinary people; in doing so, Oprah dispelled many negative stereotypes. She normalized transgender people more effectively, and with more respect and tenderness than anyone else at her level in the public media, letting her viewers see transgender persons as accomplished professionals, family persons, or otherwise gifted, talented, and well-balanced. We are also finally seeing the emergence of a few prominent actors who are actually transgender, playing transgender roles. Laverne Cox played the role of Sophia Burset in the television series *Orange Is the New Black* so well that she was chosen to feature on the cover of *Time* magazine on June 9, 2014, under the heading "The Transgender Tipping Point." She stands tall, elegant and beautiful; there's nothing pathetic or unconvincing about this woman. We are also beginning to see prominent transgender women athletes and models, alongside more troubling transgender examples such as Chelsea Manning, who was convicted under the Espionage Act in July 2013 after releasing to the public a major hoard of classified documents. Wikipedia has finally begun to use the correct feminine pronouns in its coverage of Ms. Manning, but her photograph remains confusingly and inappropriately male. Shame on Wikipedia, an organization that asserts its caring values. At least Ms. Manning found a reprieve from her harsh sentence and absurd incarceration in a men's military prison, in the final days of the Obama administration.

From my perspective, the worst transgender stereotype of all is the assertion that we're not real, or authentic, or genuine. We're accused by some of pretending to be something we're not, often couched in arguments along the lines of "God doesn't make mistakes." To my own deep chagrin, well-known feminists such as Australian-born academic and writer Germaine Greer have asserted—and continue to assert—in the strongest terms that transgender women like me are "not women."[6] The audacity of our claims of authenticity provokes many people, who in turn seek to place themselves in judgment of our being, who diminish us as irrational, confused, or mentally incompetent, or assert that we're pursuing a very selfish, fanciful fiction or "lifestyle." Some people are more narrowly focused in their bigotry and ignorance, worrying that we may be using the "wrong" public toilet room, and in more and more cases this has become a heated political debate filled with fearmongering and disinformation. After a concerted campaign in Houston, Texas, in which transgender women were portrayed as "disturbed men" and as sexual predators in pursuit of young women and girls, a referendum on an anti-discrimination ordinance known as the Houston Equal Rights Ordinance (HERO) was defeated on November 3, 2015. Because of that vote, transgender persons in Houston continue to be legally barred from using public toilets other than those which align with their gender designation at birth. The last time I was at the George Bush Intercontinental Airport in Houston to change to a connecting flight, I took a selfie of me outside the women's toilet room, and posted it on Facebook with the text "Shame on Houston!"

The expanding debate about accessing toilets is demeaning, and has become even more prominent as North Carolina legislated that we be required to use only those public restrooms that align with the gender marker on our birth certificates. Some people seem to find the public toilet situation either sufficiently vexing or amusing to stimulate them to write letters to the editors of major newspapers. Such letters pick up the

6. See Radhika Sanghani's excellent article "Germaine Greer Defends Her Transgender Views and Starts Another Row," in *The Telegraph*, dated April 12, 2016.

old trope that transgender people are sexual predators who stake out restrooms to abuse or harass young women. Other letters publicly muse over the apparent irrationality of "men dressing as women" to stand in much longer lines at the women's restroom. In early March of 2014, a woman lawyer in the Maryland suburbs of Washington, DC, marked the occasion of ongoing deliberations by the Maryland State Senate on the pending Fairness for All Marylanders Act (which ultimately did pass) to write the following letter to the editor of the *Washington Post*:

> *What a boon the Fairness for All Marylanders Act will be for female theatre-goers. Rather than waiting in an interminable line, hoping not to miss the beginning of the next act, women need only assert that they feel they are really of the male gender to take advantage of the always-shorter line for the men's room.*
>
> *While the language of the act requires "consistent and sincere expression of sexual identity," who is to say when that begins? Certainly not this legislation. As women take advantage of this law, there will no doubt be even fewer men in the men's room line.*

The writer couldn't have been more exemplary in trumpeting her own ignorance and arrogance in this cynical attempt at humor, but clearly she felt that transgender people are neither authentic nor deserving of basic respect. In the most forgiving of interpretations, such sentiments attempt to find humor at the expense of a small and generally silent minority; at worst, they are hateful and malicious words. In all cases, it's unacceptable. As I have done so often, I wrote my own letter to the editor in response, which the *Washington Post* also published.

My life as a transgender woman will continue to be plagued by people with very confused notions about who I am, based on stereotypes that simply do not reflect transgender realities. Many of the stereotypes are not intentionally caustic, but there remains a great deal of misinformation in American society about who we—transgender people—are. Even within the lesbian, gay, bisexual, transgender, queer, and intersex (LGBTQI) movement,[7] there are many who believe that transgender women are just hyper-feminine gay men, and that transgender men are the extreme end of being a butch lesbian. Again and again, I explain to people that sexual orientation and gender identity are different phenomena, yet from the persistence of this misunderstanding I don't think I'm making much progress.

As someone over sixty years old, society reckons that I'm at the upper end of middle age and that spares me from the worst sexualization stereotypes, Caitlyn Jenner (who is a year older than me) notwithstanding. Many Americans decided long ago, however, that younger transgender women are all about sex. They see young transgender women as prostitutes or sex workers, not understanding that for many such women there are no other viable ways of economic survival. They see us as flamboyant drag queens, which only a very few of us are; certainly not me or any transgender friends I know (of any age). Since American culture assumes most people over sixty are "past it" or asexual, I'm spared the worst accusations that transgender women are sexually perverted, predatory, or pedophilic. In reality most of the younger transgender women I know are shy, caring, and like all of us deeply stressed by the long ordeal of overcoming imprisonment in the wrong bodies. Given such personal histories, the stereotype of transgender women as hyper-sexual, sexually deviant, predatory, or morally questionable threats to society is nonsensical, and profoundly offensive.

What about cross-dressing? In the old days, transgender persons (particularly those moving from male to female) were pejoratively termed

---

7. In the United States, the prevailing norm is now to use the "LGBTQ" acronym, where "Q" represents "queer" or "questioning" (or both). Internationally, however, the "LGBTI" acronym is far more common, where "I" represents "Intersex." Increasingly, the acronym most preferred is becoming a combination of both, or "LGBTQI."

"transvestites," commonly understood to mean a person who dresses in a style or manner traditionally associated with the opposite sex. I still find well-meaning people using that derogatory, anachronistic term when they try to weigh in with some comment about transgender issues. It's seldom worth explaining that I've never seen myself at any point of my transition as being either a transvestite or a cross-dresser; I was just dressing in my clothes like any woman would. Rationally, it might be construed that I was unintentionally a cross-dresser all those years I was wearing boy clothes! In any event, I'm hugely relieved to be unburdened of male clothing and would never deign to put it on again. The day that the Goodwill truck drove away with my entire wardrobe of boy clothes was one of the best days of my life.

There are people under the transgender tent who derive meaning and pleasure from gender tourism, experiencing what it's like to play the role of another gender out in the world. I don't think there's anything wrong, threatening, or harmful about those who cross-dress, but no doubt it does make some people very uncomfortable. Frankly, neither cross-dressers nor I owe a comfortable life to others; none of us do. Generally, cross-dressers have no intention of irrevocably changing their gender identities, and their excursions across the gender divide are transitory and often only symbolically persuasive. I've met and talked with many cross-dressers, but not being a cross-dresser, I still don't understand what motivates them to do what they do. I don't need to understand; I respect their right to experience that particular adventure.

Cross-dressers, transgender or cisgender, gay or straight—I'll admit that it gets complicated. I've frequently detected a look of bewilderment and consternation on the faces of people I've spoken with about my life as a transgender woman. More than a few people have surprised me by concluding that once a transgender person pursues a gender transition (which doesn't necessarily entail surgeries), that person really doesn't have a *genuine* sex at all. Take it from me, being de-sexed by others isn't any fun. In the minds of too many people we've somehow become processed persons, or "transgendered" (an absurd addition of an "-ed" that removes us from being men or women). In my case, I've known that I'm a woman for a very long time, even if I did not always have the right words to describe this awareness. Transgender isn't a noun, and being a transgender woman doesn't diminish being a woman; it just says something about my history. My sex is female, and my gender identity is as a woman. Other transgender persons identify as women, men, genderqueer, Third Gender, Two-Spirit, Hijra, and other genders. Who are you to tell me—or them—that we are wrong?

Stereotypes can be intentional, even strategic. As the recent election season made clear, transgender persons are also a convenient scapegoat for the ills of the world, and some politicians have been quick to exploit this scapegoating opportunity. Among the slate of those initially competing for the 2016 Republican presidential nomination, Senator Ted Cruz of Texas took the occasion of a heinous attack in late November 2015 on a Planned Parenthood clinic in Colorado Springs to brand the killer of three persons as a "transgendered [sic] leftist activist." Another candidate, Dr. Ben Carson, described transgender status as "the height of absurdity" and said that our demand to be able to access public toilets that align with our gender identity was "beyond ridiculous." Sadly, there was little public outcry in response to these vicious characterizations,[8] and in the case of Ted Cruz's assertion, the perpetrator of the Planned Parenthood attack was certainly not transgender.

---

8. An important exception was Senator Orrin Hatch, a prominent Republican who on July 20, 2016, at the Republican National Convention in Cleveland, Ohio, strongly admonished Dr. Ben Carson for his pernicious characterization of transgender persons.

We are not predators, murderers, absurdities, or imposters. We are not "beyond ridiculous." We simply—but emphatically—claim ourselves as whole persons, and no one is better qualified to know us. So yes, we're self-ish, but not selfish. Knowing the difference matters.

STARDUST, GOLDEN, AND FIRED

In what may have been an intentional last fling prior to starting college, I drove my Honda CB 350 motorcycle on a long and unrushed summer trip through the beautiful state of Vermont, and then down into southern New York. On August 16, 1969, I drove into the Catskills on State Route 17, passing right by Bethel. Just a very short distance away, the Woodstock Festival was in full swing—and I drove right by. Unlike Crosby, Stills, Nash, and Young's portrayal in what became the anthem of that era, I was feeling neither stardust nor golden. I was in a funky mood, the weather was threatening rain, and it just didn't seem important. A lost opportunity to be sure, but I'll stay with my claim to be a member of the Woodstock generation. I'm proud that my high school and college years were characterized by a firm if naïve conviction that my generation was indeed going to change the world for the better. My friends and I would talk late into the night about peace, about meaning in life, and about community. We were all feminists, pacifists, and some of us were even toying with the notion of being anarchists. The Born Again Christians were crusading across American campuses, and I would go along to hear what they had to say. I also listened to the political talk, which was everywhere: glorious notions about ending poverty, supporting civil rights, and stopping war. My friends and I read books and discussed them fervently, and we were catholic in our literary tastes. I recall impassioned conversations about Robert Kennedy's *Thirteen Days*, Ursula K. LeGuin's *The Left Hand of Darkness*, Philip Roth's *Portnoy's Complaint*, and Kurt Vonnegut's *Slaughterhouse Five*. No one talked about making money.

I completed my college education in England, and when I returned to the United States in 1976 and moved to Eugene, Oregon, it felt like I had come home to a country I barely recognized. The hippies had fled to the backwoods of Oregon and Vermont, college students everywhere were enrolling in business programs and focused on honing their competitive skills so that they might aggregate personal fortunes, and even the language of feminism seemed subdued. There was considerable pressure to get a good job in a respectable career, and to "get on" in life. While not abandoning my values, and while feeling a genuine affinity for the hippies I regularly saw in backwoods Oregon, I was perceived as being among the respectable ones. I had already qualified as an architect, with numerous professional suffixes appended to my then-male name, and I used these qualifications to good effect when my spouse (from my first marriage) and I made the rebellious and patently naïve decision to move to Kenya. People assumed our idealism would come unstuck through such a grand but foolhardy adventure, but within three days of arrival in Kenya in June 1979 I already had five job offers. I accepted one, and happily settled into doing architecture in East Africa. More importantly, I began an unintended education in multiculturalism, and I began to open my eyes to see the places where ideals ran aground against the shoals of human failings, corruption, bias, and ambition, amidst a backdrop of grinding poverty, warmly hospitable people, and remarkable natural beauty. Within a year I had discovered that my boss was falsifying charges to institutional clients to inflate revenue, and I chose to confront him about this. He quite literally threw the book at me (but missed), and I was fired on the spot. It was the first such job termination, and there've been two more since then.

Given my career's unpredictable trajectory and the wide variety of job roles I've filled, that number may not be unusual. I began my career in the United States, but over the decades that followed I worked in far-flung locales, only returning to a more settled existence in my native Maryland in 2006. Employment in five different countries, in various capacities, in pursuit of international development and human rights projects in over forty countries isn't exactly a straightforward climb up the career ladder, especially when that globally dispersed progression of jobs was interrupted by breaks for advanced education in London, Washington, DC, and College Park, Maryland. It did not make me wealthy.

My initial fifteen-year career in architecture was carried out almost entirely outside the United States, designing and overseeing the construction of buildings in England, France, and in many African countries. In fact, my only building of record in the United States was the first actual building of my architectural career—a small school bus garage in the tiny town of Crow, Oregon. When my career shifted from the architectural profession to town and regional planning, the door truly opened to becoming a practitioner in international development. That's a very wide doorway; over the two decades that followed I embraced projects in conflict mitigation and peacebuilding, in anticorruption and leadership training, in gender equality and women's empowerment, in good governance, and in decentralization. When, much to my surprise, I became an Obama administration political appointee to the federal government, my attentions were drawn to democracy strengthening and the human rights of LGBTQI persons abroad. It's been a diverse career so far, filled with many meaningful accomplishments around the globe—and I'm not finished yet. In between these various permutations of identity and focus, of advanced degrees and overseas placements, I've engaged in no small degree of reflective thinking on where I'm going, where I've been, and why. I've labored in the for-profit sector, the non-profit sector, and government, and each offered their own variations on the pursuit of that central mission and linked identity I've long cherished: making the world a better place. There have been ups, and there have been downs.

Oh yes, and in the middle of all of this, I changed gender.

For someone whose career is anything but ordinary or stable, it's hardly a surprise that situations occur that lead to involuntary job loss. Each loss of employment seems to entail an intense sense of injustice— and a rankling irritation at the manifest impunity for the three persons who, at their respective moments in the drama of my life, decided to be rid of me. My identity has perhaps been too closely linked to the job I've been doing, the position and responsibility that I've held, and my own perception that each job provided an essential platform to cultivate my ability to pursue those old Woodstock-generation ideals: make positive, worthwhile, durable changes in the world around me. Earlier idealism and naïveté notwithstanding, I have also felt a healthy respect for personal economic security. For someone now with no savings and only minimal assets, who cherishes a simple and uncluttered life, I've been reasonably successful in the judgment of some of my peers. Others are not so sure, as they look askance at me and return to planning their comfortable retirement years and their next cruise. Whether my lack of savings (the byproduct of paying for a gender transition, exacerbated by long bouts of under-employment), and my long struggles to secure new full-time employment, allow me a future life of any degree of comfort or dignity remains to be seen. I am anguished by doubts, and I lose much sleep thinking about it.

As so many people my age are prone to saying, the time has gone by so quickly. I've been at it for over four decades, not counting those early summer jobs, first hauling sod and cutting grass on the college grounds crew and then later sanding and painting gigantic hydroelectric water pipelines for the local electric utility. Yet even there and then, the camaraderie of my fellow workers (and they were all fellows, as was the norm in those days for manual labor jobs) and the feeling of being bone-tired at the end of a long day of intense (and very "manly") physical labor under a hot sun was ennobling in its way. In each job I worked, I never doubted that those who hired me got their money's worth. Both my parents exemplified an ethos of hard work and commitment, as do all of my siblings, and through the unquestioning adoption of their lived values I never had a job (well, maybe one in the very early days) where I did not give it my very best. The idea of actually being fired was never something I gave a thought to, being imbued with that all-too-American conviction that hard work and dedication would inevitably meet their just rewards. At the end of many years of employment, I was convinced that I would do like my parents and grandparents had done before me, and retire to a life of financial security and well-earned rest.

In my case, no such Elysian field awaits me—I've taken too many risks, lived in too many insecure settings, and covered the cost of changing gender by tapping into the only source of funding available to me at that time: my modest retirement savings. Now there remains no financial cushion to retire on. For me, it'll be *work until I drop* or through ill health I, regrettably, become someone else's burden—all the more reason that finding a job has meant so much to me, as does staying employed. My next full-time job really has to see me through. The alternatives do not warrant contemplation.

Thinking back to each of those three terminations, it's difficult to avoid taking unto myself the mantle of innocent, undeserving victim at the hands of immoral, venal, or otherwise corrupt or incompetent employers. My ego has done its best over the years to insulate me from any blame for each of those losses of secure and mostly happy employment, yet who I am and the decisions I have made have had their consequences. In any event the cloak of victimhood is an itchy one, and hardly a garment I choose to wear. I certainly did not view myself as a victim when I confronted my Kenyan architect employer in Nairobi in late 1979 to challenge him regarding the fraudulently inflated invoices he'd been sending out to the client I'd been assigned to design a new seminary for. The consequences in that case were immediate; while I was visiting a friend's office the next day the Kenyan police tracked me down and detained me. My former boss had pulled the requisite strings to encourage my rapid deportation from the country, lest I spill the beans to the good Irish priests that they had been overcharged. The police informed me that if I would agree not to consult a lawyer, they would only charge me with a minor offense and all would be well. If, however, I opted to demand access to a lawyer, I would be deported on a plane that very night. My entire sense of purpose, not to mention my very modest but total financial assets, were embedded in Nairobi and would not be extricated from me in a police station over an afternoon. I agreed to forego the legal counsel, but the promise of an easy way out by the police was a sham. Instead, I was promptly charged with violation of a work permit (a charge totally without merit, having that morning received a new tourist visa and not having worked since my dismissal). I was convicted that very evening, and given a three-thousand-Kenyan-shilling fine (equivalent to just over 400 USD at the time). In 1979 that was the largest such punishment on record in Kenya, and it is a comment on my lack of deep pockets that it pretty well cleaned me out. After paying that fine, I would have been promptly and unceremoniously expelled from Kenya for having stood up to a corrupt but politically well-connected architect who had previously employed me, but I was rescued by an eleventh-hour job offer. It came from the US State Department's on-site project manager, Jim Lovell, who asked me to assist him in overseeing the final design and construction of the new American Embassy in Nairobi. That job offered sufficient diplomatic insulation that I did not require a Kenyan work permit.

In relatively short order, that State Department job elevated me to take on the overall responsibility for that project, including a significant architectural redesign, and for the next three years I presided over the construction of the building that sixteen years later, on August 7, 1998, would fall prey to terrorists' bombs. The loss of life was severe, including some Kenyans I knew and truly grieved for, but I take modest comfort in knowing that we built that structure to a very high standard of strength; the number of fatalities in this inexcusable tragedy would otherwise have been far worse.

If not counting once being laid off along with all staff when the shareholders of a large British environmental, architectural, and landscape architectural firm decided to close down their London branch office where I was the director, it would be thirty years after the Nairobi termination that I came to be fired once again. A well-established international development firm in the north of Washington, DC, had hired me as Stephen, but they fired me as Chloe. I was deemed an embarrassment, and I suppose in their worldview I was.

Following that termination, I filled the year with a variety of short-term consulting assignments, punctuated by seemingly countless commuting hours. I felt numb, my self-esteem was at an all-time low, and the future looked bleak. It only took one day to turn that around, when an unfamiliar voice on the telephone invited me to interview for a job I had never sought—to be a political appointee of President Obama's administration. That initial interview at an elegantly hardwood-paneled office at the State Department was followed by six others at the US Agency for International Development in a recruitment screening process that was poorly managed, disjointed, and undirected. I was more relieved than surprised when the job offer finally came fourteen months later, for an opportunity that completely redirected my future in ways that were nothing short of miraculous. When I left that job almost three years later, of my own accord, I left with a sense that I had just carried out some of the most valuable and meaningful work of my entire career.

The last time I was fired was without doubt the most painful. I was nearing two years at a job that was the best fit of any job I'd ever held, serving as vice president for global programs with America's oldest human rights organization. It was a job I adored, affording me deep satisfaction in the principled work I helped conceptualize and oversee. The job was a natural follow-up after the human rights and LGBTQI work that I had carried out while a political appointee, but unlike working for the government I was free to express my views on issues that were of pressing concern to me and my new employer. I enjoyed the many opportunities to advocate in public for issues I felt deeply committed to: freedom of expression, freedom of assembly, gender equality, freedom of the Internet, and the human rights and social inclusion of LGBTQI persons. I also had the privilege of overseeing a remarkable team of committed and tireless individuals who implemented the world's largest program of emergency assistance for human rights defenders under threat, mostly in countries in conflict or under harsh authoritarian rule. Day after day at that job, situations would arise that allowed me to draw upon my long years of experience to the benefit of the shared mission, and the work that I oversaw went from strength to strength. I was able to work alongside the other program-based vice president, Bobby, who has been a friend and admired professional colleague for many years and whose passion and principles have always been and continue to be an inspiration. The president of the organization was almost entirely focused on fundraising and on public political advocacy against (mostly Russian) authoritarianism, which consumed all of his time and left him with little opportunity to attend to the programs side of the organization. My vice presidential colleague and I carried on to the best of our shared abilities, and the programs thrived. By securing a significantly increased level of grants despite intense competition, we generated important and often life-saving impacts around the world, while simultaneously bringing in the funding that kept the organization afloat.

In due course, the organization's president decided to resign and move on to a new opportunity on the staff of a prominent Republican senator. Being summoned to his office on his penultimate day on the job was unexpected, but even more surprising was his intent: to fire me. Given a legal provision all too common in the United States, many organizations including this particular human rights organization employ people on an "at will" basis, which allows them complete discretion to fire people whenever they choose, for any reason—or for no reason. Under these terms, such employers bear no requirement to justify such life-wrenching decisions; it is arguably an odd stance to adopt—legally and morally—for an organization committed to human rights. While he did not mention the fact that I had made it to the finalists' stage in the competition to replace him as president, he did assert that I had been too engaged in the promotion of the human rights of LGBTQI persons, and he stated that my open, quiet, but steady internal advocacy to make the organization a leader in human rights and democracy in the context of gender equality was misplaced and unwelcome. In neither case were these assertions supportable, but he wasn't inclined to discuss this; the decision had been made and what I had to say was simply filling time. I left that room convinced—as I remain to this day—that I had been fired for reasons that had everything to do with who I am as a transgender feminist, and nothing to do with my proven competence and demonstrably excellent performance as a senior executive.

There remained the choice to try to fight back, and I did make an effort to reassert my human dignity while staying resolute in the identity I knew to be genuine, and the record of performance that I knew to be accurate. It's a tactic for the confident, in which you demand that you be valued on the job for that which you have accomplished and contributed, as well as for your demonstrated record of personal integrity. While this direction offers a transgender person more empowerment, it's extremely difficult to sustain in the face of power exercised by supervisors who are adversely inclined, with lawyers all too willing to impugn your reputation, and with a convenient "at will" clause to fall back upon. The practical options for the transgender person in such a situation are few, except to cling tightly to what those in power are unable to wrest from us—the sense of who we are and the conviction that at some point justice, decency, accountability, and basic civility will come to characterize our relationships on the job.

We're certainly not there yet.

MADAM PROFESSOR

The beginnings of my gender transition affected more than my full-time employer. I was also on the adjunct faculty of three universities in the Washington, DC, area, usually teaching one course per term, alternating between the three campuses. For the fall term of 2008 I was teaching a graduate course at the School of Public Policy at the University of Maryland, and in the late summer I had already coordinated with them on transition arrangements. The School of Public Policy was helpful and very supportive, and their matter-of-fact acceptance enabled me to begin that fall term teaching *en femme*, even though it was a few weeks before I went one hundred percent into Chloe mode in the remaining components of my life. The first class of that term was on September 4, but I was delayed in Florida caring for my elderly father, so my dear friend Bobby agreed to teach that first class. Bobby and I had both been in senior management positions from 2003 to 2005 at an international development and foreign assistance organization whose offices were located on a flotilla of house boats in the Potomac River, not far from Washington's famous Tidal Basin. I would come to work closely with him again from 2012 to 2013 when we were both vice presidents at my last employer, and he remains among my dearest of friends.

Bobby had met me as Chloe for the first time in August of 2008, at a lunch at a Greek restaurant in the Dupont Circle area of Washington, DC. Before going full-time in Chloe mode, I'd made selective excursions in the anonymous urban world of Washington, starting with drives in the car and graduating to travelling on the metro system. No one paid me any notice at all, much to my relief and delight. I took considerable pleasure in simply seeing my feminine reflection in the metro car's windows, and in the anonymity of being just another woman. Through such adventures, my confidence in engaging with the world as my authentic self was increasing by the day. Still, meeting Bobby at that summer lunch was a very big step for me. I needn't have been anxious; Bobby is a true mensch. He rose to greet me with a hug at the restaurant, and throughout the lunch he was unfailingly warm, gentlemanly, supportive, and bursting with amiable curiosity. It felt wonderful!

Later, after substitute teaching that first class for me at the University of Maryland in College Park, Bobby related to me how nervous he'd been that he would mistakenly refer to me as "he" or as "Stephen" when speaking to my new students. He made himself a large sign on a sheet of paper that had the words "Chloe" and "she" written on it, and placed it where he could see it but the students could not. He doesn't recall making a single gender mistake, but he admitted that he was perhaps more focused on not making such mistakes than on the topic he was teaching.

For so many transgender women, the existence of a voice in the masculine register feels like the most insurmountable obstacle. Unlike the testosterone-induced voice changes that provide transgender men with persuasively masculine voices, being on estrogen makes no impact whatsoever on transgender women's vocal cords. They've already been stretched to male resonance from decades of testosterone, and overcoming this requires learning to pitch one's voice upwards in what is termed "forward resonance" and "modified intonation." To me it felt like I was talking into my sinus cavities, but it began to make a difference after many hours invested in voice therapy lessons. I started these lessons initially in June of 2008 at the Speech and Hearing Center at George Washington University. Compared to almost any other transition expense, at fifty dollars per session this was a relatively affordable program. A very pleasant and professional graduate student named Melissa worked directly with me, overseen every so often by Linda, a speech-language pathologist and clinical supervisor. Under their combined tutelage my initial progress was modest at best, but the two important takeaways had little to do with feminizing my voice. First, I was fascinated to overhear Linda discussing me with Melissa, and referring to me using feminine pronouns. That was the first time in my life I'd earned the S; all at once I was "she."

Both before and throughout my transition, I was bedeviled by anxiety about whether I would "pass." Would I be woman enough? While hardly a suitably dramatic setting for a momentous and triumphant achievement, my true test came in June 2008 when I entered a woman's toilet room for the first time, there at the Speech and Hearing Center. Perhaps bolstered by the apparently unselfconscious choice of feminine pronouns employed by my speech therapists, and humbly aware of the growing urgency of a call of nature, I pushed the door open into the women's restroom, dreading the possibility that a woman might be in that room. My worst fears were realized; an elderly lady was just washing her hands. For me the moment of awkwardness seemed to stretch on for minutes, but thankfully the anxiety belonged only to me. She barely looked at me. I had unwittingly placed my validation at the feet of this unknown woman, yet in being so inconspicuous I had "passed." No trumpets sounded, no certificates were issued, and no new coins were minted to commemorate this event. I didn't know whether to feel comforted or embarrassed, but fortunately I had other matters to attend to.

Impatient for better voice results faster, and knowing that my job entailed extensive public speaking, I sought a new voice therapist. I was fortunate to find my way to a remarkable woman, Tish Moody. Tish had coached opera singers, was able to describe speech techniques that made sense, and had the distinct benefit of having worked extensively with transgender women. She is also a caring and supportive person, and under her guidance and through some very intensive work on my own, I began to make reasonably good progress. I can remember practicing on an old cassette tape recorder on my drive in to work each day and back home afterward, replaying my recordings over and over and over to hear if I was progressing. It probably wasn't the safest thing to do while driving, but it was one of the only spaces where I had relative privacy to vocalize to my heart's content, as loudly as I dared. Thanks to that practice, and with the kindly but demanding tuition of Tish, I was soon ready to tackle that first class.

My first teaching experience came on September 11, and I showed up early after carefully dressing and adjusting my wig (while waiting for my own hair to grow out). I looked reasonably good, but my biggest concern was still my voice. These classes each went for two and a half hours, so sustaining my voice in a higher register and projecting that voice (unamplified) out to a class of twenty students over that extended time period was going to be a challenge. Staying safely sheltered behind the teacher's podium wasn't an option either; I needed to be as close to the students as I could be, so that they could hear me.

Somehow that first evening went by with no embarrassing moments or gasps of incredulity among the students. As became a common experience in so many later encounters, I never quite knew whether people accepted me as simply Chloe, or accepted me as a transgender woman named Chloe. In either interpretation, what mattered was that they accepted me, and each class thereafter became progressively easier. No one was ever scandalized! If my voice occasionally sounded curiously low or uneven, the twenty grad students either failed to notice or were too polite to remark on it. In time I hit my stride, and haven't had a single disconcerting voice moment since while teaching. I taught all the classes that followed being poignantly aware that I was defining the success of my own gender transition—very much a work in progress at that time—as being about convincing other people that I was not a transitioning transgender person. The unfortunate slang expression, "passing," makes it appear that we are getting away with something fictitious or insincere instead of achieving a threshold of acceptance that allows us the space we need to get on with our lives in the gender we know ourselves to be.

Both of the other universities with whom I was affiliated were also wonderfully supportive when I informed each of my transition, which occurred at the same time that I let my full-time employer know. Administrator (and now Assistant Dean) Leslie Evertz, of what was then the Georgetown University Public Policy Institute (now the McCourt School of Public Policy—where I still teach periodically), in particular wrote back almost immediately with very kind words and reassurances that they would do all in their power to be as supportive as they could. The School for Advanced International Studies of the Johns Hopkins University was similarly responsive.

On the heels of having been fired at the job where I transitioned, and despite the receptivity in my world of adjunct teaching, I needed a full-time job. The next few months were very unsettling as I struggled to find work. Adjunct teaching would pay only a few of my bills, but every one of my many applications for full-time job openings was unsuccessful. I hadn't anticipated there would be such resistance to hiring a transgender woman, but I was forced to conclude that this attribute was probably the primary cause of my poor job-search results. Given my well-developed technical skills and extensive global experience, I should have been a formidable candidate—had I not been transgender.

FAITH, ETHICS, AND LEADINGS

Photograph by Benjamin Verdi, Grant Thornton LLC

AUTHENTICITY AND OATMEAL

Before I can tell my life what I want to do with it, I must listen to my life telling me who I am.

—Parker J. Palmer, *Let Your Life Speak: Listening for the Voice of Vocation*

Listening is what Quakers do. I've lived too many lives that were not mine to lead—lives that led me to very dark places—until the wisdom, light, and corduroy sensibilities of Quakers such as Parker Palmer taught me to stop and listen. Quaker listening is directed inward as much as it is upward; that essence of the divine is right there inside. I had only to open myself to its message, and listen. Maybe I wasn't expecting that inner voice to be female, but then again . . .

Being true to my self-ish nature is another way of saying that authenticity matters. Authenticity was important to me long before I began my gender transition journey, but with that journey it took on a depth that eclipsed any earlier understanding I may have held to. Authenticity also happens to be a central theme in Quakerism, and in my own values—two categories which are converging more and more all the time. Being immersed in Quaker sensibilities, convictions, and community, I frequently forget that we Quakers are a tiny and (to some) even quaint religion, best known for a smiling face on an oatmeal container. That association is ironic; it was adopted as a very successful brand by a nineteenth-century Christian evangelist and philanthropist, Henry Parsons Crowell, who was not a Quaker. I am not surprised that some people think of us as an anachronism, or express surprise to learn that we still exist.

Claiming our continuing presence doesn't convey who we are as Quakers. That's a confusing task, because we're characterized perhaps more for our diversity than for any common creed or articles of faith. We may be better known for our belief in the centrality of a faith community, a belief which for me was to prove instrumental to the success of my transition.

All who are associated with the Religious Society of Friends, as Quakers are formally known, trace a common origin to the turbulent mid-seventeenth century of Britain, when many peace churches emerged. From that origin, nearly all Quakers would be likely to describe their faith as one in which access to the divine is available to every person, and need not be mediated by or through a member of the clergy (although some branches of Quakerism do have pastors). We don't try to define what "the divine" is, often simply referring to "the Light." Probably most adherents of my faith would also concur that how we live our lives as Quakers is far more important in describing our faith than are any words we might offer, even though as a faith, most American and British Quakers don't proselytize. For Quakers, our authenticity is probably best evaluated in the consistency of our actions and our principles, religious or secular, and in our commitment to speaking truth to power. "What cans't thou say?" is a Quaker challenge from our earliest days, charging each of us to align our life with our faith and values. It's a challenge that is directed as much to ourselves as to others.

My first awakening to Quakers was when I learned of their courageous and principled stance against the Vietnam War, and against the forced conscription of young American men that supplied so many warriors for that conflict. It wasn't until I was living in London in 1990, however, that I found my way into a Quaker meeting. As so often happens for Quakers who come to this faith in their middle years, I felt immediately at home.

Westminster Friends Meeting in the heart of London, adjacent to Trafalgar Square, provided me a nurturing and congenial community, blessed with some spiritually *weighty* older Quaker women whose wisdom and caring guided me at a very vulnerable time in my life. My decade in Africa was over; I'd just left my home, career, friends, and a failed first marriage in Kenya and was making an all-out effort to settle into a new architectural career in London, find new friends, and create a new life. At Westminster Friends Meeting I came to know remarkable women who became important spiritual mentors in my life. Hope Hay Hewison was an author who had once lived in South Africa. She often spoke eloquently about issues of the day and persons in her life, in a manner that was consistently and effortlessly framed by her Quaker values. Of the same generation, there was also Audrey Wood, whose self-effacing manner endeared herself to me. Her mentorship and remarkable spiritual insights led me ten years later to advocate for naming my own daughter Audrey, which thankfully my spouse consented to. And finally there's Diana Galvin, now quite elderly, but an exemplar of salt-of-the-earth spirituality and a person of unbounded caring and resilient warmth. Diana is a friend in every sense of the word, and I have treasured her affection for me over the years.

While Quakers are few, we are widely scattered. In my travels in Britain, South Africa, Kenya, Ghana, Mexico, Canada, and in many places within the United States, I've visited with Quakers and always felt completely at home with them. While they sometimes vary in their traditions and priorities, every visit has the effect of strengthening my convictions that it isn't just my beliefs that make me a Quaker. For me, being a Quaker is more about my commitment to participate in a genuine spiritual community of listeners, each of us staying intentionally open to discerning a divine will, and giving our best efforts to live our lives in harmony with that discernment. It can be a truculent and even unlovable community at times, but it is my spiritual community.

Quakers do come together around a number of shared testimonies, which bear some reflection in the context of my own life journey. These testimonies offer one vantage point from which to consider both personal and global challenges, but before weighing in on these pressing concerns, Quakers generally wrestle with a preliminary question. Should religion focus on the realities of this imperfect world (and, in my case, my previously imperfect embodiment within it) or instead give priority to some world to come?

For most Quakers, Eden isn't history. Eden exists, but at a deep, ineffable level. It's not commonly perceived by Friends as a primordial world order in which a unity of purpose and harmony once thrived, but instead many of us perceive it as a foundation of original vitality and integrity that we can still connect with. The spiritual lens of Quakerism is both selfish and world-affirming, and offers a remarkably healthy and inclusive perspective for one on a journey across genders. The shared testimonies of my faith include simplicity, peace, truth and integrity, community and equality, and stewardship of the environment; each of these testimonies has a central place in my wholeness and in my journey.

Simplicity takes many forms in Quaker life. For most Friends, living a life that is as uncluttered as possible by material possessions and the noise of trivial distractions allows us to be more attentive to listen in silence for the spiritual leadings upon which we depend. Simplicity also expresses a level of solidarity and opens a door to a better understanding with those whose lack of material possessions is not a matter of volition, but of economic reality. Finally, leading lives that are simple allows the richness of common humanity to express itself more fully and more directly, in all genders and sexual orientations. To some extent, simplicity has been thrust upon me as my economic resources have dwindled, but I have never been attracted to a life of clutter.

The Quaker peace testimony relates to a view of a world in which—through concerted peacebuilding actions—the reasons for war will cease to apply. Early Quakers were called Friends of the Truth, and although that appellation is no longer in use, Quakers frequently still refer to each other as Friends. The Quaker testimony of Truth and Integrity challenges Quakers to avoid duplicity and hypocrisy, to honor promises, and to speak from conviction, even in the face of powerful opposition. Being honest to my convictions and my sense of what is authentic, and living my life in an honest effort to achieve that level of integrity, is a spiritual discipline that underpins my transgender journey and probably even made it possible.

Community and Equality can be compared to a cosmopolitan moral perspective, in which the moral worth of all is held to be equal, anywhere in the world. Even in the England of the 1640s, Quakers adopted what was then a radical position in their belief that women and men possessed equal spiritual authority and moral value. Now we are challenged to take that conviction beyond a binary view of gender. The testimony of Equality is also pertinent to issues of social inclusion amidst diversity, avoidance of exploitative social, economic, and political relationships, and the embrace of an increasingly multicultural and diverse world. We need to get beyond "the other" and see that—in all the most important aspects of being human—we are all one.

In our own stubbornly outspoken ways, Quakers are often agents of change within secular society. As described above, our Quaker testimonies have direct bearing on the repugnance of discrimination against transgender persons. Such discrimination is a global problem, and even here in the United States only seventeen states and the District of Columbia have laws to protect transgender persons from discrimination. Those laws vary in their coverage and effectiveness, but I feel that vulnerability—particularly in light of the recent political upheaval in this country. I struggle to understand how it can be that so many people of differing faith traditions and beliefs choose to remain silent about the plight of transgender persons. As transgender people, we are either of little interest to, or strategically exploitable (at the margins) by, the politically and culturally powerful. As Quakers we view our world with our eyes wide open, and don't pretend that the current world order and the recent American political change is benign for disadvantaged minorities such as transgender persons. Quite the opposite; Quakers often feel called to find nonviolent means to confront powerful institutions of intolerance, violence, oppression, injustice, ignorance, and occasionally malice that underpin these negative forces.

On a personal level, my Quaker faith has been and continues to be a strong guide to my transition. Being authentic to my discerned gender means listening inwardly for a clear calling to resolve the dissonance, to create wholeness, to be present as myself to my family and friends, and to open the door to integrity and keep it open.

The door to integrity is of course a metaphor. This particular door to integrity leads to a room behind. I've often described my personal "door to integrity" as analogous to living in a home where I perceive there's something amiss; the proportions don't feel right, the corridor is just too long. At the edges of my consciousness, I play with the idea of a room that the builders never completed and just sealed up, but in my metaphor I know that it's an absurd notion. Absurd, until the day comes when a door I'd never seen before is simply there, in the middle of that long corridor. I summon my courage and open the door.

Inside, the room is lively, sunny, and very feminine in its appointments. Pink wallpaper? Perhaps not. What's most memorable, however, are the multitude of drawers and cupboards—some ornate, some simple, some enormous, some very tiny and intricate. Each drawer and cupboard is an invitation to discovery, and I sense that in each I will find a part of the Chloe life that is now available to me, to be aired and incorporated into my story, my life. The contents of some drawers are playful and frivolous, while in others there are heavy challenges and profound leadings. Of course the room also boasts a beautiful gold-rimmed mirror, in which I see my reflection as Chloe with a clarity and wholeness—integrity—that I have never before experienced. It's a glorious room filled with light, warmth, and softness, and I know that it is now there for me—with abundant discoveries still to encounter and reflect upon—for the rest of my life. It will take me more than that long to open each drawer and cupboard, and to be present to what each contains. Naturally the contents of these drawers and cupboards defy material description. Much of their content is symbolic, even ineffable. Call them elements of the soul; these are the spiritual essences that contain meaning, identity, and warmth for this self-ish Quaker woman called Chloe.

One Sunday in 2010 a woman in my Quaker Meeting in Adelphi, Maryland, felt moved to rise and speak out of the silence, as Quakers sometimes do. In her message, she talked about what she called "thin places" that we all experience in our lives—places and situations where we feel only thinly separated from some great meaning, some great significance, and occasionally, some great peril. She described how those thin places are sometimes the reward for something that we've sought for a long time, but how at other times the thin places are encountered when we're being challenged by something hard, sad, or mysterious. She described being present at a birth or a death as examples of thin places that we all experience at points in our own life journeys, where the separation between us and divine meaning or miracle is very thin indeed.

Her words had a deep resonance for me. After a long period of weighty silence in the meeting, I found myself on my feet, as a message moved through me. My words described an image that had come strongly to me, filling my mind. It was an image of crossing an icy river—of being challenged to get to the other side, but having to deal with thinness along the way. In my message I shared the metaphor of a river, and the knowledge that my life lay on the mysterious other shore, even though it meant leaving all the comforts and familiarity of my own shore—all the "thick places" that had allowed me to live a relatively easy life. I was drawn to the far shore, but as I crossed the frozen river I could hear the danger signs of cracking ice underfoot. It was getting thin, and the water was deep and turbulent below. Finally, I got to a point where the ice felt remarkably thin, and was ready to give way. I lacked the courage to go on, but then I noticed that others dear to me had also joined me on this crossing. They had places—ways across the river—that were parallel to mine and also thin, but not thin enough to break. They were close to some deep significance in their own lives, and confronted their own sense of peril and risk, but their paths were not my path. We are all on spiritual journeys, not just those of us who are transgender.

Even as I spoke aloud to the meeting, I found my moment of grace. I knew that my path was to fall through the thinness, and to trust the waters below. I had to believe that the waters would actually be warm and life-giving, and that I would rise from the waters reborn, to continue to the other side with my spirit—my soul—transformed and ready for what awaited me there. The challenge was to have that faith, and to hear the cracking of the ever-thinning ice as an invitation and not a threat. I knew that I would step forward, and give myself to the fall. And the waters would be warm, and comforting, and transformative.

As you might imagine, that message offered a very strong—even mystical—sense of the journey I'd embarked upon. Taking that fall in reality was when I finally came to understand that authenticity and meaning came from accepting that I am a woman, that I am Chloe, despite the dangers that the cracking of the thin ice portended. It was time to give myself to the journey of wholeness, to listen to where my life was trying to lead me, and to be intentionally self-ish.

SINGING MESSENGER, DANCING ADVOCATE—IN AFRICA!

Every human being brings a truth into the world. Every human being is a messen-
ger of God—not only Jesus or Buddha or Zarathustra; they know they are; others
don't know that they are. But the moment you are born you bring a truth in your
being. And unless that truth is expressed you will not feel contented. Unless you
deliver the message to the world you will feel a deep discomfort because you are not
fulfilling your duty towards existence. You have to sing the song of your heart. You
have to dance your dance. You have to be utterly individual, not an imitation, not
a carbon copy. You have to bring out your original face. The moment you are able
to reveal your original face to the world, your life will be fulfilled. Tremendous joy
arises out of it.

—Anonymous

Africa offered a grand stage upon which to try out my dance, to learn the
words and music of the song of my heart, and what being myself might
look and feel like—even if I began that dance with the wrong sheet of
music. Attracted there at the incautious age of twenty-eight, and feeling
sufficiently accomplished and confident in the progress of my architectural career to convince both myself and my young British spouse that we
could be the authors of our lives and achieve our shared destiny wherever
we chose, we saved and borrowed and sold possessions to cover the cost of
our Pan Am tickets to Nairobi, Kenya. We were left with just enough money to survive in Africa for about two weeks. As it transpired, it was more

than enough; I had job offers from local architectural practices within the first few days, and promptly settled into fulfilling a new role: expatriate professional, and "man of the world." The trappings were evocative of adventure and daring: ample time to take a first-class (yet in reality inexpensive) berth on the old-world overnight train from Nairobi to Mombasa for unrushed weekends of scuba diving; the tropical pleasures of a beautifully landscaped Nairobi home complete with domestic staff and gardener; and (in time) membership at the fabled Muthaiga Country Club. That membership included access to the inner sanctum—their men's bar—made famous by Meryl Streep's re-enactment of Baroness Blixen's brazen entry there in the 1985 film *Out of Africa*, which was filmed while I was living and working in Kenya but in a replica Muthaiga Club not far from the original. In retrospect, I suppose that my own (repeated) entries to that actual men's bar were similarly brazen, which may explain why I never quite felt that it was "my" space. Chloe had no business being there!

Kenya offered me an adventuresome young gentlemen's dream, and a singular opportunity to combine my exposure to all things British (from my years of architectural training and practice in England), my American can-do impetuousness, and my fascination with the wild and rugged wonders of equatorial Africa. There were safaris with expatriate friends deep into the bush in my clunky but dependable Toyota Land Cruiser, formal dances and lovely dinner parties, and engaging conversations with a rapidly diminishing population of aging British colonials who were an integral part of the recent history of Kenya. Having a white-tablecloth, best-china Christmas dinner (cooked and cleaned up afterward by the aforementioned domestic staff) atop trestle tables set out on the open plains of Tsavo Game Park, dressed in formal attire, and knocking back glasses of premium scotch—it was certainly unlike anything I had encountered before. If I had any feminine inclinations or subconscious awareness of Chloe, they (and she) were pushed down to an inaccessible part of my psyche. This was a man's country and a man's adventure, and I was immersed in the script of being the "*bwana*" (Swahili for man, "*mabwana*" in plural), enjoying elevated status, significant responsibility, and the choices that come with it. On "Africa time," where nothing is hurried, there were also abundant opportunities to explore, hike, camp, rock climb, and windsurf (once barely making it through a family of hippos). I might be forgiven if I thought I cut a dashing figure, as I became one with that small and very white expatriate circle. I was living large, living male, but not listening to my life at all.

Africa has its own way of teaching humility, and it isn't an optional lesson. My most important education in authenticity lay before me, but first I had to understand what it truly means to open my eyes, ears, and heart to grasp who I am. In time the unfiltered clear light of Africa even brought me face to face with the reality of being Chloe, but for that life-saving privilege I had to wait many years and pay a very high emotional price.

First, however, I had some important lessons to learn about the world. While I played among the affluent and privileged expatriates, all around me were Kenyan women, men, and children who suffered deprivation and loss of hope well beyond my ability to comprehend, or my inclination to learn about. The many countries that constitute Africa, to a degree like all countries everywhere, are each beset with extremes of wealth and poverty. For far too long I simply saw those who were among Kenya's impoverished inhabitants as backdrop, cautiously avoiding any direct recognition of their individual humanity. It took two incidents to sweep away that convenient fiction and sense the world I was in.

In 1980 my first wife was hired to be the landscape architect in a project to renovate the Kenyan Presidential State Lodge at Sagana, on the slopes of Mt. Kenya; she would later win an international award for her work there. As her spouse, I got to tag along once on a site visit. From the vantage point of President Daniel arap Moi's glamorous lodge, I had ample reason for abstracting away the more distant backdrop of pervasive poverty. After all, the sight of poverty was jarring and profoundly uncomfortable, and very much inconsistent with the tropical forest around me, alive with exuberant color and rich with sound and life. Yet poverty was never far away; even as I walked the grounds of the lodge I came upon a throng of very poor Kenyan children clustered on the other side of the tall, barbwire-topped, chain link perimeter fence. Full of smiles, wonder, and amusement at what we were doing, one young boy's eyes caught mine. He couldn't have been more than ten, yet our eyes locked in a long, warm stare. That connection was accepting, innocent, embracing, joyful, and deeply human; an exchange that negated countless differences of culture, age, relative affluence, education, personalities, and gender. I was sad at the time that I hadn't learned the boy's name, but I have since come to cherish his anonymity. He could have been anyone, and in a way he has become for me *everyone*—the essential common bond that all humans share when we are open to that sharing. On that day so many years ago, I felt his unique humanity as I am sure he did of me; from that point onward the challenge of reconciling my life of privilege amidst stark poverty became both deeply personal and spiritually irresistible. I still carry that young boy in my heart and mind, as I reflect on the human dignity that shone from within him. Somehow the Indiana Jones manly swagger suddenly lost much of its allure, as I learned essential lessons of compassion and solidarity.

The second wake-up call took the form of a tall, smartly dressed Kenyan teenager of perhaps eighteen who sidled up to me as I walked along a street in downtown Nairobi, one afternoon early in 1981. My original inclination was to ignore him, assuming he was a panhandler or that he otherwise viewed me as a tourist—an easy target ripe for exploitation. Sadly, he seemed all too aware of my remoteness and the reason behind it, and he promptly reassured me that he bore no ill intentions, nor was he seeking any money from me. He had a lovely smile and spoke excellent English, which he used to reassure me that his only reason for approaching me was to discover if I were American. I confirmed his supposition, and he then told me that he wished only to offer me his gratitude on behalf of all Kenyans. "No," he stopped . . . "on behalf of all Africans."

Now I was transfixed: What could possibly be the cause for such a communication, much less justify me to be its recipient? He proceeded to explain that when my president, then Jimmy Carter, had defended the human rights of all human beings everywhere, he and his friends felt embraced and honored. "I want to thank you that your president—the president of the United States of America—is a champion for *my* human rights, a Kenyan." It was all he had to say, but his wide and warm smile communicated a sincerity that left me first feeling proudly patriotic, but quickly had me wondering what it all meant. Why had my president said such words? Where did I fit in to that message, and what was it all to me? I'm still searching for that answer. Being in Kenya suddenly was more than just an exotic adventure; it was to become a profoundly reflective journey with a moral awakening that began at that very moment.

Eight years later, on the heels of a failed marriage and the closure of my own economically unsuccessful architectural practice, I left that expatriate life in Kenya with my emotional treasury nearly bankrupt, and my moral awakening still a work in progress. I would have more to pay emotionally before Africa was through with its lessons. Another six years later would find me traveling from Washington, DC, to Durban, South Africa, with my second wife and our three-month-old son Ian, to step into the role of managing director of a new joint venture between my US-

based employer—a very large global engineering firm—and a local engineering firm. The new entity was called Siyakhana, which in Zulu roughly
translates to "working together in harmony." Siyakhana was a new town
and regional planning firm, and my change of career represented a professional progression not unfamiliar to many architects. Both professions
challenge their practitioners to integrate and harmonize complex systems
and in so doing achieve desirable results; for the town planner, however,
the end goal is not the creation of a building, but instead the satisfaction
that comes with facilitating sustainable and popularly supported development for a community. Being new to South Africa, I was more than a little
aware that I had much to learn in a very short time. Ever the optimist, I
assumed my new role with energy and confidence. To my pleasure and
great relief, Durban was also the home of two of my very best friends,
Jenni and Dan Smit, whose Afrikaner lineage had not stood in the way of
their courageous role in supporting the African National Congress and its
aims throughout the years of the anti-apartheid struggle. Jenni and Dan
warmly took us in and helped us to adapt to our new environment, and
their two daughters, Alexia and Olivia, delighted in spending time with
our very young son.

South Africa in 1995 had a remarkably different feel than Kenya.
While being white, professional, and presenting as male still conferred
status and privilege, the aura of the all-knowing expatriate was nowhere
to be seen in this port city. In Durban there were very few Americans or
other foreign residents from developed economies; indeed, many white
South Africans were emigrating as fast as they could to the United States,
Britain, Canada, New Zealand, or Australia. These were turbulent days in
South Africa just after President Mandela had assumed power, with the
future of the country very much in doubt. Racial tensions were always
present if just below a veneer of civility, but as an American I was consid-

ered somehow unencumbered by my pale complexion—I wasn't viewed as a personal accomplice to the troubled legacy of apartheid or colonialism. Black South Africans were much easier to befriend than black Kenyans had ever been, although the cause of that alienation from Kenyans had much to do with the separation and aloofness of my earlier Nairobi expatriate life.

The work I was to undertake in Durban was audacious, collaborating with South Africans to spatially reconfigure and heal those parts of South Africa that bore a deep, ugly thumbprint from earlier planners. Such planners had fulfilled the apartheid dream by segregating land use by race; they had also designed road layouts specifically to control access, thereby ensuring that potential disturbances quickly could be contained. Siyakhana emerged right in the middle of sweeping national change, as we facilitated processes that allowed very different people from across the economic, racial, social, educational, and gender spectrum to come together in "development forums" to air their respective and often conflicting arguments on how South Africa's development funds ought to be spent. My colleagues and I had to learn to listen, to make sense of it all, to feel both the pain and the aspirations of people forged by years of struggle, and then to somehow translate it into policies and action plans. Africa was busy teaching me again.

In retrospect, the hubris of a white American architect—suddenly turned town planner—coming to Durban to help orchestrate a complex redesign of South African physical realities under conditions far more about cacophony than harmony is astounding. Once again, just who did I think I was? While shaped and seasoned by the many hard lessons of poverty in Kenya and throughout eastern Africa, and by my exposure to the multiple development challenges of many other African countries I had already visited on project work, nothing prepared me for the South Africa of 1995. My demeanor was far more subdued than in my decade in Kenya; I had begun to take notice of my emotional sensibilities as I listened and learned as quickly as I could. Many friends and professional colleagues helped me, not the least being the aforementioned Dan Smit—regarded as one of South Africa's preeminent town planners. Dan graciously agreed to serve as chairman of Siyakhana, and his wise advice and my growing openness to listen to such wisdom saved me from many missteps. A South African engineer named Dean Barnes, with a prodigious record of having designed and implemented cost-effective ways to bring basic sanitary and water infrastructure to very poor communities, also provided invaluable support and guidance. Along with an intensive process of learning the ropes while being accountable to the two firms who were the demanding joint investors in Siyakhana, I was also pursuing the intensive lessons of what parenting meant. Christine had not been to Africa before, and frequently being stranded alone at home with a young child made her feel insecure, unsettled, and underappreciated. While I struggled to play the masculine role of competent, *high-powered* American executive backed up by the vast resources of a global engineering giant, I was losing the struggle to do justice to the lovingly masculine roles of husband and father. Priorities became skewed, and our marriage suffered extraordinary strains. Keeping the veneer in place became progressively more unsustainable. I wasn't listening to her, and I wasn't listening to my life. I also wasn't listening to the Chloe within, yet she was making her presence known more and more each day.

Our son Ian attended a moms-and-tots play group that, because of white South African social conventions, was not open to dads except on rare occasions. One such time was at the annual Christmas holiday gathering, and Christine, our son Ian, and I were the only ones there who weren't South Africans. Everyone was pleasant and conversational, but my favorite moment came when we gathered outside on the stone patio with the children to sing Christmas carols. Only then did I notice that every South African dad present had made his way upstairs to drink beer with the lads and watch the rugby on the television. Still, I was oddly aware that I was just where I was supposed to be, with the moms and tots, and I relished every minute of it. It was one small example of listening to my heart, listening to the Chloe within, and tapping into the joy and meaning that flowed from that special—if largely still muffled—source.

Our three years in South Africa exposed me to deep development challenges and possibilities, as South Africans taught me the sophisticated skills of effective public participation processes. Again and again in such gatherings, the issues that were most daunting were not the technical demands that planners are trained to take note of and be responsive to. Instead, those in the participatory workshops spoke of their aspirations, their dreams for a safer and happier future with ample opportunities for their children to grow and prosper in a multiracial society. Again and again, the participants in such workshops asked why the poor were poor, why the politicians were corrupt, why the women had no voice and few resources, why the perpetrators of violence against women and the poor enjoyed impunity, and why the whites still enjoyed disproportionate power and wealth. They asked what was to be done to make amends for years of suffering under apartheid, who was responsible for opening doors to the jobs and choices that still remained closed to them. They spoke a great deal about human rights and about the values so eloquently stated in their constitution, and—using human rights language—they asserted demands for fairness and justice. I felt mute, but I listened intently; I had never been trained to address such overtly moral concerns. Given the gravity and moral force of their claims, and their insistence that under the emerging new South Africa they be afforded the rights and freedoms that any dignified human being ought to enjoy, I keenly heard their passion but also knew that I was out of my element. They were asking questions at the heart of what "development" ought to mean, and I had no answers. The patina surrounding my role as managing director of Siyakhana faded. That role began to feel hollow, my manly focus on professional performance felt less and less persuasive to me, and the pressures of my progressively unhappy marriage convinced me that it was time to change. I still wasn't ready to understand and embrace my authentic self, but I knew all about reinvention and playing the next manly script. So I set about the task of reinventing myself yet again—in effect to avoid once more listening for the challenging messages that lay at the core of who I was. We left South Africa in June of 1998, and two months later in Maryland, I began doctoral studies in applied ethics and public policy.

It isn't fair to describe my four years at the University of Maryland's School of Public Policy as an all-encompassing distraction, although at times it felt so. Halfway through my studies we had a baby daughter, Audrey, and home life became busier—happier too. The children were their own wonderful distraction, and I found tremendous pleasure in continuing to immerse myself in certain parenting roles. Reading books at bedtime, lots of rambunctious playtime, presiding over most bath times; the pattern of bed-play-bath provided stability and pleasure and kept me from losing myself irretrievably in the world of the intellect. I invited my young son to participate in the redecoration of his bedroom, and together we chose wallpaper border trim embellished with motorcycles and bright colors, and he even "helped" me with the painting. We built elaborate structures out of Lego blocks and popsicle sticks and straws, and he joined me every summer in preparing, planting, and harvesting our small vegetable garden (leaving the weeding to me!). We collected and played marbles, and obtained pet goldfish (in ever larger quantities, in ever larger tanks—which I always somehow ended up cleaning). Together we would snare fireflies in small insect-catcher containers, and marvel at their glow. As Audrey became more mobile and independent, she would join our activities, bringing her own personality into everything we did. Yet even before she could crawl or walk, she was part of many shared childhood adventures. At the tender age of seven months, she made her Halloween mark *trick-or-treating* in an adorable M&M costume as Christine and I carried her around the neighborhood, with a costumed Ian and his friends at our side. Bath time was particularly fun for both children, with all manner of toys for them both to play and splash with, and seldom any hurry to rush the process.

Still, my doctoral studies demanded extraordinary time and effort, even if they were fascinating (if you don't count the economics classes), and I benefited from the remarkable mentoring of the renowned philosopher, Professor David A. Crocker, who chaired my dissertation committee. By the conclusion of that dissertation I was comfortably fluent in and enjoying the application of the language of ethics and public policy, including but by no means limited to human rights. Having only Christine's income for two years, and then the addition of very modest income derived from my part-time employment for the following two years, incurred enormous financial pressures on our family. Between the demands of balancing our budget and becoming adept at moral theory and its application, there was little time or resources for any other pursuits—like reflecting on my own identity, or listening for inner guidance. Still, I was becoming more acutely aware that by allowing myself to be distracted, even if for justifiable reasons, I was still running away from a confrontation with myself about myself. It would require that confrontation to take place and be resolved—by far the biggest challenge of my life—before I could circle around to using my skills as an ethicist to reflect upon what it means to be transgender, and more importantly, to be authentically myself. That has come to include much thinking through the question of whether there exists a human right or other persuasive moral basis upon which transgender persons can be justified in claiming a gender identity contrary to that which they were assigned at birth.

Before I could attempt an answer to such questions, I had to give some thought to what "gender" is, and that really only became my priority after my gender transition. It was then that I became aware that no consensus exists; prominent gender theorists such as Dr. Judith Butler have explained gender as something that is produced and performed, or more accurately that is produced through repeated performance.[9] In her view (one most thoughtful transgender persons reject, myself included) gender emerges through a series of "acts" repeated by a person, and is always subject to further changes. To Butler, gender is conceptualized as repetitive social fictions that are created and built up over time, which in turn are embodied as "truth" or perceived as "natural" through the performance of what she termed "social scripts." From Butler's perspective, gender is *performative* but gender doesn't express any inner or subconscious sense of identity—which is directly at odds with the sense of identity described by most transgender persons who feel so moved as to change their assigned gender identity. It's an interesting theoretical debate, but in most developing countries the gender identity dialogue isn't articulated in terms of "performative" versus "natural." Instead, gender is culturally imposed and not subject to revision on any terms. Any attempt to deal with internal gender dissonance by rejecting your biological sex assignment and having the audacity to redefine your own gender identity and associated roles will leave such persons open to verbal assault, moral recriminations, exclu-

---

9. For further details on Judith Butler's thinking, I would recommend her 1988 piece "Performative Acts and Gender Constitution: An Essay in Phenomenology and Feminist Theory," in *Theatre Journal* 40, no. 4 (1988): pp. 519-531, and her 1990 book *Gender Trouble: Feminism and the Subversion of Identity*, published by Routledge.

sion, humiliation, or even violence. Such a beleaguered position is hardly a strong one from which to assert human rights claims.

Any moral consideration of such a claim must first begin with an assessment of whether "gender identity" is a clearly defined moral category. No one doubts that multiple and often conflicting perceptions of masculine and feminine exist (gender expression), but disagreements really come to the surface when we consider whether certain universal moral values ought to be assigned to or at least be more closely associated with "male" or "female" (gender identity). The situation gets even more complicated when the basis for gender assignment itself is open to moral questions—i.e., who has the right to assign a person's gender identity and upon what basis?

As if the definitional and listing-authority questions regarding gender were not complicated enough, what constitutes authentic gender? Ought gender be considered within a binary structure, or should gender lie upon a gender continuum? There are even people—and I am not one of them—who reject the notion of gender categories altogether, and seek to be respected as dignified but ungendered human beings. Others make the moral (and often legal) case for a third gender which may or may not be defined to include (some) transgender persons.

For my own part, once I made significant progress in pursuing the arduous reflective work of coming to terms with my inner identity, I wished to be recognized—socially and legally—in the only gender identity that feels authentic, even if this entails enormous risks in my public presentation. I believe many transgender persons wish the same for themselves. For persons like us there is no acceptable option, and no closet to escape into. If we persist in the public presentation of an assigned gender that we know to be inauthentic we will experience the excruciating discomfort of gender dissonance. In time, such duplicity is simply unsupportable. It's neither an exaggeration nor melodramatic at that juncture to describe my necessity to transition as a matter of life or death, and for many transgender persons that is a common threshold experience. I'm left with no doubt that continuing as Stephen would never have seen me through to the current year.

Universal human rights begin with equality, freedom, and dignity. Gender isn't an equivalent foundational issue for most people, but it was—and is—for me. Those of us who constitute a relatively tiny minority at the fringes of society have a different and more vital relationship with gender. I know, and I've heard transgender friends express similar convictions, that my gender authenticity is so hardwired into my "self" that a life in the wrong body—wearing the "wrong face"—would be no life at all for me. If I and those like me cannot own our individual humanity, wear our own faces, and be respected as persons of equal dignity to all others—even if we are transgender, gender nonconforming, or intersex—no other human rights matter for us.

It doesn't get any more basic than "self." Unless we are self-ish, we are not present in this world.

If that line of thinking and the actions that flow from it lead to wearing the label of a human rights and social inclusion advocate, that's a label I'll wear with pride and determination. The roots of my advocacy for human dignity stretch back to my upbringing, to my extensive work as an international development practitioner, and to my scholarly endeavors in learning and using the persuasively strong human rights and social inclusion language, and the versatile vocabulary of ethics. No doubt, too, that my identity as a human rights and social inclusion activist was shaped by the direct integrity challenges I've faced throughout my unfolding gender history, and through coming to know and care for many human rights defenders globally. There are remarkable transgender and allied voices around the world speaking out strongly in support of the human dignity of transgender and intersex persons. There are also many allies of transgender human rights defenders outside the international LGBTQI community, people who've taken a committed stance to support transgender persons and our human rights claims.

One such ally played a big part in my African education. Professor Byaruhanga Rukooko is a warm and energetic philosopher who became a steadfast friend in 2005–2006, my pre-transition year as a Fulbright senior scholar at Makerere University in Kampala, Uganda, and he has remained my firm friend throughout my transition. On numerous occasions, formally and informally, he's joined with me in public outreach and in intellectual endeavors to raise awareness of the human dignity of all marginalized persons. Once, when I—as Chloe—returned to Kampala while still a political appointee of the US Agency for International Development (USAID), Rukooko accompanied me to a presentation to the Ugandan staff ("foreign service nationals") of the US Embassy and USAID Mission there. The goal of the session was to explain to the Ugandans (and to those American staff who also chose to attend) why the US government supported the human rights of LGBTQI persons. While fully aware that this wasn't a popular topic in the toxically-homophobic environment of Uganda, I thought that the gravitas of my senior stature in the US government and my usual ability to project a demeanor of likeability and trustworthiness would win hearts and minds. Instead, some of the Ugandans in attendance were openly alarmed and distraught by my promotion of the human rights and social inclusion of persons whom they generally felt to be despicable, ungodly, even subhuman. The mood in the room became less than cordial, and what civility remained deteriorated completely when I acknowledged that I, a woman, was (then) married to a woman. Loud argumentation and unruly accusations ensued: of my un-Christian behavior, of corrupting Uganda's children, and of exporting Western moral decay. The situation was dramatically exacerbated when I made the unwise disclosure that I was not just married to a woman, but that I once had been embodied as a man. The atmosphere in that room, in the heart of the American Embassy surrounded by employees of the US government but in the very middle of Africa, suddenly felt confused, perplexed, hostile, even bordering on threatening. At that juncture, the distinguished Rukooko—a man held in very high regard by Ugandans as a senior academic—walked up to me and calmly put his arm around my shoulder. He looked out at his fellow Ugandans in the room with a quiet yet intense authority. After first clarifying that he was neither gay nor transgender, he simply said, "I am Chloe's friend." He did not have to say anything more; his face said it all. The session was over, but my friendship and respect for this courageous ally was forged unbreakably and forever. Africa had taught me another lesson.

My USAID appointment in October of 2011 had been to a new position, as Senior Advisor on Democracy, Human Rights, and Governance to USAID's Africa Bureau's Front Office. Within two weeks of starting, however, my job description also included helping USAID—agency wide—to articulate a clear policy position on the human rights of LGBTQI persons around the world. And while that Ugandan experience was the most edgy during my three years as a political appointee of President Barack Obama's administration, the very fact of being the first transgender political appointee in the history of any US foreign affairs agency or department was, itself, central to my subsequent human rights and social inclusion activism.

In the federal government the promotion of policy positions and standards is a common duty of many senior political appointees, but that promotion is clearly limited to specific talking points that delineate the administration's official position on a given topic. In short, at USAID I was speaking for the government, not for Chloe. Fortunately for me, my advocacy priorities with respect to democracy, good governance, and the human rights and social inclusion of all persons—including but by no means limited to LGBTQI persons—made sticking to the official talking points quite easy. The opportunities to speak were not limited to tense gatherings such as the one at the US Embassy in Kampala. They included three days speaking and guest-teaching at Dartmouth University in New Hampshire, several other one-day university visits, and a major conference of political scientists in San Diego (together with my aforementioned friend and colleague, Prof. Rukooko, on his first and only trip to the United States). I also spoke at two high-profile presentations at the White House, and once at the presidential retreat at Camp David. Public speaking comes easily to me, helped in no small measure by the long process of feminizing voice therapy that my outstanding voice coach had seen me through. Still, as much as what I said and the way in which I said it, the simple fact of being wholly present as a transgender political appointee— and simply of being transgender—was and remains a strong message.

This was particularly so during travel to meet senior government officials in developing countries. Until we figured it out, those of us on the USAID delegation were befuddled at the realization that such visits often were marked by very high attendance at only the initial meeting. In time we solved the riddle; the senior government official's staff had Googled the background of the visiting USAID delegation and it was easy to find out that one of the distinguished visitors—me—had a rather unusual history. Most of the "surplus" attendees of these initial meetings were there to gawk, but they never stayed the full course of the meeting. As a well put-together and articulate woman of a certain age I offered no sensational or scandalous news value to them. One of my senior USAID colleagues began to refer to this as the "Chloe moment" of these bilateral visits, and he mused that the impression of a transgender woman carrying out a sophisticated and responsible role in an effective way may have been the most durable advocacy contribution of each of these visits.

In those days, my primary connection at the White House was Brian Bond, who was then the deputy director of public engagement while also serving as the White House's LGBTQI liaison. On his initiative, he held monthly meetings of all three DC-based transgender political appointees: Amanda Simpson of the Department of Commerce (and later the Department of Defense), Dylan Orr of the Department of Labor, and me. Having a very senior White House official asking probing questions each month about how the Obama administration could do more for transgender persons domestically and abroad inspired me, as did Brian's evident personal concern and commitment. When Brian left to take a position as the Democratic National Committee's director of constituency outreach, his successor held these meetings irregularly, and then not at all. And now—well, the improbability that the new administration of President Trump would ever deign to appoint transgender persons, much less convene them at the White House on a regular basis to seek their input, says all one needs to know as to why I am a Democrat.

My focus on human rights and social inclusion however did not start with my political appointment. There is a continuity in my own human dignity narrative that has propelled my advocacy for human dignity internationally across my international development career, whether it's been for downtrodden Filipinos compelled by their culture to accept their poverty and powerlessness, or for the dignity and rights of Ugandan widows who, upon the deaths of their husbands, had stood powerlessly as their children and lands had been reallocated to male relatives of the late husbands. I have advocated in Mexico City on behalf of and in solidarity with desperate Mexican parents whose demands for information about their "disappeared" college-aged children went unanswered by corrupt and callous Mexican police acting in league with narco gangs, and in Washington, DC, and Nairobi, Kenya, for threadbare and hungry Somali civilians with vacant gazes and little hope, displaced by seemingly never-ending conflict. The global assault on human dignity and rights proceeds apace on so many fronts, but I hold a special place in my heart and in my advocacy for transgender people and the whole LGBTQI community around the world.

While domestic human rights advocacy hasn't been a focus of my career until recent political events forced me into something of a reorientation, I did once before pursue advocacy in my own state of Maryland through supporting that prolonged quest for recognition of the human and legal rights of transgender Marylanders—for people just like me. On March 4, 2009, I stood in front of the relevant committee of the Maryland State Senate as they took testimony regarding Maryland Senate Bill 566. This bill's title was awkward but clear: Human Relations—Sexual Orientation and Gender Identity—Antidiscrimination. After waiting a very long time for my turn, I stood at the podium and explained—in the scant three minutes allocated to me—that my advocacy in support of this bill was seasoned and shaped by my status as a transgender woman and by my strong sense of my civic duty as a citizen of Maryland. I acknowledged the political realities at the outset—that the state senators really had no pragmatic reason to support our cause. We're few in number, so our direct voting power isn't a factor and our plight isn't likely to attract the attention of most citizens, many of whom don't even know we exist. Of those who do know, a proportion of them are only drawn to us for the wrong reasons, out of prurient fascination. Some Marylanders simply find the idea of us repugnant, while others feel compelled to honor their own moral and spiritual beliefs: to support such a bill would have been tantamount to sanctioning "deviant" behavior. They listened, wondering what I was driving at.

Jumping from politics to morality is ambitious in three minutes. I asserted that gender identity is fundamental to being human, and that discrimination against us as transgender persons denies our basic human integrity and negatively affects our ability to care for our families. I even quoted from the respected professor of philosophy and African American studies, Anthony Kwame Appiah: "Our moral modernity consists chiefly of extending the principle of equal respect to those who had previously been outside the compass of sympathy; in that sense, it has consisted in the ability to see similarity where our predecessors saw only difference. The wisdom was hard-won; it should not be lightly set aside."

For transgender citizens of Maryland, State Senate Bill 566 would have cleared away much of the discrimination in employment, housing, credit, or public accommodations (including public restrooms) that assaulted our dignity and frustrated our efforts to find a life of meaning. The potential to live a truly human life of dignity, free of shame, rests in large measure with every person's freedom to express their deepest convictions of their own gender identity. I argued that the state should embrace the concept of gender identity in this context, and provide the legislative framework that reflects these common but important values.

My time was almost up, but I quickly returned to Professor Appiah for one more brief quote: "What's age-old is that when we are asked—and ask ourselves—who we are, we are being asked what we are as well." Looking straight at the state senators, I asserted that *what* we are is simple. We're human beings and citizens of Maryland, and that is all that must be known about us. *Who* we are is, however, complex—each of us has a story, a life, hopes, and aspirations just like any other citizen of Maryland. All that we were seeking was to be treated in like manner, free from discrimination in employment, housing, credit, or public accommodations. My time was up.

The bill never made it out of committee that year. It would not be until March of 2014 that my home state of Maryland finally passed such a bill. Maryland then joined sixteen other states and the District of Columbia in protecting the rights of transgender individuals from being discriminated against in terms of access to housing and jobs, along with other forms of exclusion. As for transgender persons in those other thirty-three states, they remain unprotected and disrespected, often at great peril to their well-being and aspirations. And now, in a wave of extreme conservative push-back sweeping this nation, twenty-nine state legislatures are considering the imposition of "bathroom bills" like North Carolina's. If I travel within this country, I may soon have to learn yet another womanly skill: how to pee in the woods.

Still, there has been significant progress in achieving human rights protections and freedoms for lesbian, bisexual, and gay Americans, as the momentous Supreme Court decision on June 26, 2015, making same-sex marriage legal across this nation demonstrated conclusively. The momentum of this victory may be enough to carry over to improved rights for transgender Americans, although with Trump in the White House this conjecture may be premature. It is equally plausible that gay, bisexual, and lesbian Americans and their allies may feel that their work is now accomplished, and they may withdraw from further activism. We will only know through the passage of time. In the interim, the plight of transgender persons in the United States is only marginally improved (although violence against transgender women of color appears to be worsening), and in developing or repressive countries it remains bleak and as poorly understood by the general public there or here as the meaning of "transgender" itself.

The creation of standards of governance that are responsive to universal human rights and respectful of universal human dignity remains a distant goal. Even though I and nearly all transgender persons know or at least sense from an early age with uncanny (if often hard-to-articulate) clarity that the gender that we were labeled with at birth was wrong, despite the sexual characteristics of the bodies that we occupy, this is all very awkward for those in authority. They don't know me or other transgender citizens and may feel they have no need to learn. We are few in number, and our stubborn pursuit of nonconforming gender identity often makes the general public uneasy. The transgender phenomenon also outrages many religious and cultural leaders (sometimes spilling over to mobilize hordes of extreme-right Internet trolls) who all fill the Internet and local media with caustic diatribes against transgender persons, cloaked in religious certitude and smug deprecation. In governments, those in authority would rather ignore the rights-based demands of transgender persons, as modest as such demands are. If pressed to do so by transgender activists or their allies, such authorities are prone to react in a punitive and repressive manner, hoping to deter or intimidate these odd persons who have had the temerity to make their day so uncomfortable—odd people such as me, Chloe.

If only they knew that it's uncomfortable for us too. Having a brain that knows it's in the wrong body is a tough concept to explain, especially since our claims for recognition of authentic gender identity almost always get conflated with the sexual orientation issues of lesbians, bisexuals, and gay persons. As I have noted earlier, all transgender folk get called gay, and in more than seventy-eight countries that label can lead to detention, arrest, or worse.

In a world replete with human rights abuses affecting vast numbers of people, the curious and awkward misfortunes of those with mismatched bodies—transgender folk like me—seem insignificant. Perhaps viewed through the blunt utilitarian calculus, that's true. But when we dare to be self-ish, to stand up for the fundamental right just to be ourselves despite the audacity of transgressing that previously impassable barrier between the sexes and all that this barrier means, we make a powerful statement that human dignity matters.

OWNING A PAST, RESTARTING A LIFE

Photograph by Alexandra Milentey

REINCARNATION

Every so often I've been asked whether I believe in reincarnation. Sometimes the questioner delves deeper, before I've even answered the first question, to ask whether I was a woman in any past life. I will admit to having experienced one very uncanny (yet disappointingly ungendered) feeling when I first visited Berlin, Germany in 2014; it felt very much like I had been there before but not in this life. That anomaly aside, I have no particular reason to suppose that reincarnation is plausible. Still, I'm attracted to the question as it relates to my (current) life, including identifying what aspects from my own personal history might cohere over the years as *identity.* Is it even possible to draw together many past chapters of one's life under one recognizable and persistent sense of personhood? Is this a search for one's soul?

Metaphysical or theological musings aside, the construction and discovery of personal identity is at the heart of being me—and through that identity convincing the world that I am who I assert myself to be, in whatever gender feels self-ish. Life is never static; the knowledge that those fifty to seventy-five trillion cells that together constitute Chloe have differing life spans and are variously replaced (or not) as we age leaves the biological question of a residual or consistent identity unclear. Perhaps I should be comforted to know that brain cells do typically last a lifetime, and arguably the intellect is where my identity resides. Or is it? That brain-body divide is no longer persuasive for me; I feel a very reassuring new sense of oneness with my now female body and I hold a conviction that the totality of Chloe has never been more integrated. Perhaps claiming that present wholeness is casting the historical person who was known as Stephen into an odd and ambiguous space of incoherence: Who and what was Stephen as a small child, a teenager, a young adult, or as a middle-aged person? Where was Chloe all that time? There are no clean and simple answers, but there are patterns that emerge.

Upon reflection, my life and its many patterns do seem to subdivide more or less neatly into ten "past lives." These are more clearly defined in my evolving career pursuits, and although the Stephen-Chloe question wasn't always in evidence, these ten past lives can be very briefly summarized in the following set of recollections:

Infancy and Childhood

I was a relatively carefree youngster, the middle of five children, with loving parents and a secure and stable family life. Yes, we moved every two to three years, as military families often do, but since I was surrounded by other military families this transient life seemed normal. My dad was away fighting in the Korean War for two years early in my life, but otherwise he was almost always nearby, and we were a tight and caring family. We had our own traditions and adventures, deep ties to my dad's family in southeastern Ohio, and nearly as strong ties to my mother's family in and around Clearwater, Florida. I have some memories of very early life in New Orleans (where my father was a Marine Corps recruiting officer), but it wasn't until I was in second grade in Southern California that I first sensed that I was not much like my brothers, and that my mom was my more comfortable role model. No one seemed to mind. I remember being very close to my mother throughout these early years, and also taking a special interest in helping care for my baby sister Barb (ten years younger than me) once she appeared on the scene. With a very busy mother and a house full of children, taking on the responsibility of mother's helper to care for my sister felt like a real calling.

Military School

The security and relative tranquility of my life was rudely and dramatically changed in eighth grade, when the family moved to Wisconsin for my dad's own renegotiation of his life as a retired colonel. He softened the separation from his Marine Corps career by being employed, at his first post-military job as Commandant of Cadets at a military academy. There he continued to wear his uniform and to hold firmly to his identity as a senior Marine Corps officer. While he worked at the academy, my brother George and I were cadets based in the halls of residence ("barracks") of the academy. We were rarely able to see our family. These two years were a perplexing time of deep unhappiness for me, as I struggled to make sense of the hyper-masculine environment and the attendant loneliness and separation from my family. I remember a sense of profound disconnect from all around me at that academy, made worse by knowing that my parents, younger brother, and younger sister lived only a short distance away on the edge of the campus. I was expected to "man up" and live in the barracks.

High School and College

Almost as quickly and dramatically as my world had been reconfigured to a teenage, Spartan military ethos—artificially separated from girls, women, family, and pets—I was whisked away from the military academy as my family relocated to the small New York State college town of Potsdam. There I was placed in a public high school, where I was free to rediscover myself among the integrated company of boys and girls. This new freedom became a time for experimentation, growing my hair long, wearing Day-Glo bright pineapple shirts with matching bright socks, only to later foreswear such garish colors to instead adopt a subdued, pale-green, Mandarin collar shirt. (It made me look sophisticated and exotic, I thought.) Thankfully the family was all back together again (excluding my two older brothers who were off at universities in Ohio and Wisconsin), and I was again in close proximity to my mom and my sister. I finally had an academic environment where I could—and did—flourish, in my own quiet way. While I sensed that I was in a different place than any of my male or female friends, I immersed myself in art, sewing, German and Latin classes, and in copious reading. Even when I went off to college, my anchor was that family home in Potsdam.

I did try once again to win my father's respect and to prove myself in a masculine world by signing up for the Reserve Officers' Training Corps (ROTC) at Rochester, but the clash between being an art student (which I adored) and wearing that Army cadet uniform at the height of campus protests against the Vietnam War was unbearable. My ROTC career lasted only two weeks.

England and Oregon

I seized the opportunity offered to me by Syracuse University to do my last year as an exchange student at the Architectural Association School of Architecture at Bedford Square in London. I learned more about politics, polemics, Marxism, single-malt whiskey, the proclivity of English motorcycles to drip oil, illegal house-sitting (squatting), and being self-sufficient than I ever learned about architecture at that school. Yet it was a place to mature and become more worldly, and to take advantage of what London, as a great world city, could offer. And England taught me what it meant to be an American—a lesson that is perhaps only accessible from the perspective of a foreign shore. In no time at all I was an earnest convert in the ranks of international student Anglophiles on a tight budget, reveling in the sing-along Christmas carols at the Albert Hall, watching the Royal Shakespeare Company perform at the student rate of twenty-five pence, avoiding London Underground fares by jumping turnstiles, window shopping along Oxford Street, and developing a taste for a cheap pint of English bitter beer. The year went by but I stayed on, working as an apprentice architect. I had reason to stay; in London I met a beautiful young Englishwoman and surprised myself by falling almost as much in love with her family—her caring and interesting parents Julia and Donald and their pet dog Amber—as I did with her. Melanie's family home in the English countryside became my second home, and I gravitated toward her mother as she shared with me some of the domestic insights of a woman who was a consummate homemaker and a good citizen of the village, a woman who had never baked a cake (or anything) from a mix. In relatively short order I enticed my family to cross the pond for a very traditional English wedding, all the while Melanie's mother marveled at how much I wanted to be a part of designing and preparing the wedding, which she ascribed to my being foreign. Once married, my young wife and I then moved to Oregon where she completed her studies, but being in Oregon always felt like being a long way removed from any place I could call home. Oregon was a rugged and wild place, and as a newlywed it reinforced my efforts at being "the guy"—although I still felt a persistent affinity for the women in my life. Three rainy years were enough, however; we were young and reckless, and Oregon felt painfully provincial. There was a whole world out there, and Africa beckoned.

Africa and Architecture

A single Swahili class can lead to unexpected outcomes. At Syracuse University I needed another language credit, and their East African Studies program offered a course in Kiswahili. I signed up for reasons never really all that clear to me, but it left its mark. After studying Swahili, Kenya felt like a real place, and a tantalizing one. A few years after studying that language, and at my urging, my wife and I saved all our money, put our modest worldly possessions and camping gear into our rebuilt, 1965 VW Beetle we'd named Henry, and drove and camped all the way through freezing February weather from Oregon to Florida. From there we flew off to Kenya with our paltry savings. I reveled in the scale and audacity of the personal challenge, willing myself in manly fashion to make it a success, while being inexcusably insensitive to my wife's very reasonable desire for a modicum of security. At least my British professional qualifications made finding an architectural job in that former British colony relatively easy, and in no time I was well on the way to reinventing myself as the next Denys Finch Hatton.[10] This was a form of manliness that appealed to me, tough but refined. I became president of the American chamber of commerce in Nairobi, went on a camel safari, acquired an African grey parrot named Kasuku (who subsequently remained my dear companion for thirty-three years), and drove a sturdy, short-wheelbase, dark-green, 1969 FJ40 Land Cruiser across terrain of the extreme ruggedness for which such cars were made. I gave my weekends over to windsurfing, mountaineering, horse riding, or technical rock climbing. My marriage began to unravel, but I pushed myself until it all—marriage, job, intrepid Africanist persona, self-respect—suddenly slipped away. The safari-suited,

---

10. As Wikipedia states: "The Hon. Denys George Finch Hatton was an aristocratic big-game hunter and the lover of Baroness Karen Blixen, a Danish noblewoman who wrote about him in her autobiographical book *Out of Africa*, first published in 1937." Robert Redford played an Americanized version of his role in the movie *Out of Africa*, which was filmed while I lived in Kenya.

manly Stephen persona was emptied by that collapse, but in retrospect it was inevitable. Keeping up that façade had come at a very high cost to my wholeness.

Washington, DC, and International Development

There was no denying a sense of tail-between-my-legs defeat as I retreated back to live a normal American life. While comforted in the international city of Washington by the company of other former American expatriates who had been in Africa, I was newly single and I needed to engage with the world on new terms. I took up jazz dancing, which soon became an obsession, although one that I disclosed to very few people. Being in a dance leotard moving to music among mostly women dancers was a radical departure for me, but became a foundation for my future growth. I dated a few women, with relationships that always left me feeling like the relationship was more about finding myself in them than creating any bonds of intimacy—which in retrospect was probably accurate. When I met Christine, however, everything changed; she was beautiful across so many dimensions, a soul-searcher on a journey, and someone who felt instantly like a trusted and fascinating companion. We shared a deep spiritual bond that was nurtured by our Quaker community, and we became fast friends—indeed, the best friend I had ever found. In time that friendship grew into a closer intimacy and eventually marriage.

Africa and Town Planning

Still I pushed myself, and in so doing pushed Christine. To her discomfort we packed up our lives and our three-month-old baby Ian and headed off to Durban, South Africa just at the start of Mandela's presidency. I delighted in my work as a planner, but I held tight to my commitment to be home every evening. While being a parent was profoundly fulfilling for me, I was at best an uninspired and often self-absorbed husband, as the rising inner turmoil of living the wrong life became progressively more apparent. While I dearly loved my son and my wife, I simply didn't like myself. I couldn't figure out why, although it was there in Durban that I began to really connect directly with the deep discomfort of being male. I knew after three years that staying any longer in South Africa would be insupportable, and we headed home to the Maryland suburbs of Washington, DC.

Maryland, Doctoral Studies, and International Development Ethics

Before I even left Durban, I had applied and been accepted at the University of Maryland where the School of Public Policy was then co-located with the Institute of Philosophy and Public Policy. This meant I was immersing myself in an environment rich with eloquent, morally-reflective thinkers and speakers. I loved being back in the academic world, learning to apply the metrics of values and principles to the most daunting challenges of international development. After graduation I started teaching in the evenings and summers as an adjunct professor, which was a delight that I continue to this day. My family was thriving and Christine and I were doing better, until the glow wore off from the doctorate. Then the reservoir of unresolved identity issues was no longer containable, and was soon to overwhelm us both.

Fulbright Professor in Uganda

I'm not entirely sure what possessed me, but in 2004 in my fourth year of being gainfully employed in Washington, DC, at an international development firm playfully situated on a small flotilla of houseboats near the Tidal Basin, I submitted an application to the State Department to become a Fulbright Senior Scholar. Specifically, I proposed that I be based at the

Department of Philosophy at Makerere University in Kampala, Uganda. Perhaps I felt that I had little to lose by applying since I wasn't an academic and my chances of being chosen were consequently unlikely, but in due course I was indeed offered that opportunity. Our son Ian was a fifth grader, and our daughter just in kindergarten, but the year turned out to be fabulous for them both even if Audrey only remembers the essentials. It was also my first time serving as a full-time academic, doing research and teaching ethics courses to Ugandan graduate students. Our accommodation on the campus was modest, but we managed to buy a ten-year-old Toyota Land Cruiser Prado wagon in excellent condition, and we made the most of every weekend by taking "safaris" to many rugged parts of Uganda. We also took one longer trip across the border into the game reserves of western Kenya, which was an adventure replete with getting seriously lost, driving for hours with a local man who graciously volunteered to guide us. He directed us off the gravel road and up a dry riverbed through nearly impenetrable bush, but he got us safely to our destination. The Land Cruiser was tested to its limit, as was its driver (me), but in the pleasant comfort of retrospect it was all great fun.

In addition to my teaching, while at Makerere University I gathered all the materials and research notes that I would need to complete my first book, *Reclaiming Value in International Development*, which was published in 2008. By that time my transition had begun, and the book that had begun to be written by an author named Stephen was published under my new name.

Gender Transition and International Human Rights

From 2006 onward, my life has been consumed with the project of becoming self-ish. Claiming Chloe is a gender transition process that will inevitably continue to characterize whatever years I have before me. Each day is qualitatively so much richer, and I am so incomparably more at peace than before my transition, even if I am now confronting a life ahead with very few economic resources to sustain me. But I am me; I am left to marvel that all of this has even been possible—especially since I retain such close bonds with my two children, Ian and Audrey, and my ex-wife Christine, who remains my closest friend.

WHEN I WAS A LITTLE (BLANK)

"When I was a little girl . . ."

Half of adult humanity makes frequent use of that common narrative device as women share their respective personal histories. For transgender women who transitioned after their youth, these are words we are denied; our histories as wrongly embodied little girls are at best complicated and at worst awkward or painful. I've become adept at just saying "when I was young" and proceeding cautiously from there, but never without feeling a certain emptiness. What does it mean to be a woman who never had a girlhood? What does it mean to be a woman who had a boyhood (at least in some significant sense)? How does it feel for me when I watch a happy young girl unselfconsciously at play, simply being present in her girlhood? And for someone like me who is now (in my mid-sixties) the most attractive I will ever be as a woman, what must that beautiful twenty-one-year-old woman feel as she walks lightly by in her innocent but alluring sundress, a picture of feminine beauty at its apex?

Naturally, these questions aren't new, and don't only apply to transgender women. The question of any transgender person's gender history quickly centers in on their core gender identity, even if situated for many years subconsciously. I would argue that Chloe's personality, and in some ways even her beauty and femininity, were always present within Stephen.

Still, it's not comfortable for me to ponder Chloe's existence across those many decades, deeply submerged, trapped, or otherwise constrained. I am secure in my knowledge that being Chloe wasn't an invention dreamed up in my fifties, any more than decades of inhabiting Stephen's persona was fiction. While transitioning required interventions that changed my voice and my physical body in so many ways, being Chloe required no lessons. I just needed a supportive and safe space to be; the rest flowed naturally. As I transitioned into becoming fully Chloe, many previously confusing or largely faded memories from my own history returned—sometimes vividly. Often such memories—even if just about a few moments in my past—are intense.

Among the earliest is a very strong image from a sunny and warm weekend afternoon in the late spring of 1959; I was enjoying a marvelous view from high up in a tall tree. Concealed amidst the leafy branches, I looked down on the large grassy yard that was shared by the families of the dull row of officers' townhouses at Camp Pendleton Marine Corps Base in California. Between the leaves I enjoyed a clear line of sight to the festivities, as the screaming, giggling, dancing, and cavorting girls below held hands and wheeled around the birthday girl. She was my age, eight; she wore a beautiful pastel-yellow cotton dress embellished with a cute white sash in the waistline, with matching long white ribbons in her golden hair. I'm unsure if I even knew her name then, but I do clearly remember feeling that the extraordinary chasm that separated me perched alone in my tree and the *girl space* below wasn't just physical. I can also recall how much I wanted to be part of that girl space, although at that time I could not have put that into words.

My childhood is replete with many similar images, longings, and memories, although it would be wrong to say I was miserable in my boy body. I did have fun playing with my brothers and friends, yet that year—1959—

was my first conscious awareness that I was different from my brothers and from the other boys I knew. My parents tried to be accommodating in a number of ways, leaving me now to wonder in their absence what might have been going through their minds; foolishly, I never asked them when they were still alive. Each winter my parents had a habit of asking my three brothers (my sister arrived later) and me what we each hoped for as a special present for Christmas. That year I knew right away; I wanted a child-sized ironing board and an iron. My parents somehow obliged, and a brief 8mm movie clip still exists of me delighting in the bliss of exterminating wrinkles with my toy ironing set, which really did plug in and get slightly warm. Sadly, my passion for ironing did not persist into adulthood, but when I was eight it was what I wanted to do. More importantly, it may also have been an indicator of what—or who—I wanted to be.

I pushed my luck too far the next Christmas when I asked to be given a doll; my parents balked. In time they relented just enough to allow me a special doll-sized teddy bear with whom I instantly bonded. The day, however, came when I decided (with appropriate nine-year-old logic) that my teddy needed a bath. It was a fateful decision that led to the poor unwashable toy's demise, and to my consequent period of protracted, anguished mourning. Later teddy bears followed, and over the next two or three years I would dress them in colorful clothing crafted out of construction paper and glue, and have wonderful tea parties and position them in colorful parades.

Nothing unusual about my boyhood, no.

During that period between eight and twelve years I found my way to small pockets of female space, although it was never called out as such. My parents indulged me in behavior that, in retrospect, probably generated much pillow talk between them. After the family left California and arrived in the Virginia suburbs of Washington, DC, I became my mother's shadow in our small kitchen and fondly remember the two of us exalting over the arrival of the new avocado-colored refrigerator and oven. How could any appliances ever be more beautiful? My mom seemed entirely at ease to have me at her side when preparing meals or cleaning up, or the many times that I served as mother's helper in taking care of my sister Barb (or "Bitsy" as we called her then) in her infant and toddler years. My parents were very sensitive too, as when they gently explained to me that no, I couldn't be the "flower kid" for the wedding of the young couple who lived in the tiny rented apartment above our garage because that couple wanted a flower *girl*. The memory of that disappointment remains oddly poignant to this day, as it marked an end to a certain gender innocence.

Moving forward, my father and I spent more time together, and there were many talks between us about the manly virtues—talks that I can only imagine he initiated. As a US Marine Corps colonel, he was the exemplar of the "officer and a gentleman" kind of Marine, and not of the gravelly macho Hollywood variant. He never spoke of combat, although he had been active and—according to a letter of commendation he received—quite heroic in some of the most grueling battles of the Pacific campaign of World War II and later in the Korean War. He taught me, and I assume he taught my brothers too, how to be a gentleman. The social institution of "lady" was also very important to my father; his spouse adroitly and graciously met those challenging social expectations and took them to the next level as an officer's wife, homemaker, schoolteacher, and mother to five children.

As mentioned earlier, at twelve years old my world changed dramatically. My father retired from the Marine Corps, and took up a second career as the commandant of cadets at a military academy just under thirty miles due west of Milwaukee, Wisconsin. One of the "benefits" that lured him there was free tuition for my older brother George and me, since we were both of eligible age to attend that school. What small amount of girl space I had been able to quietly and unselfconsciously enjoy completely vanished as I was placed into a hyper-masculine environment as a cadet. An unsightly stone monument at the middle of the campus bore a plaque that instructed us: "Don't be a mollycoddle." Many of my fellow cadets came from deeply dysfunctional families. My first roommate (who was frequently harangued by other cadets for having the unfortunate first name of Leslie) described to me how his father had chased his mother into a closet and then used an axe to break open the door, threatening to kill her. During that incident Leslie had called the police who had arrived just in time, but his father had retaliated in due course by dispatching him to the military academy. In time he ran away from the school; I don't know whatever became of him.

In those two years my only refuge was among a very small set of gentle cadet friends, and by volunteering for acolyte duties at the Episcopal Church on the campus. I remember feeling considerable comfort dressed in the flowing robes that acolytes wore, and basking in the refuge of the litany, music, and ritual within the thick gray stone walls of Nobel Victory Memorial Chapel.

My other safe space was the dining hall. Subconsciously, I responded to my hyper-male environment by compulsive eating, rapidly gaining over fifty pounds and costing my parents a small fortune in new and ever-larger cadet uniforms. My defiance of the revered lean and muscular cadet stereotype had consequences; my obesity made my presence in the ranks look ungainly and unbecoming. Nowhere was this discomfiture more evident than at the Sunday full-dress parades, but being resourceful I volunteered to be on the cadet version of the military police. That choice allowed me to spend each of the parade afternoons helping to direct parents and siblings to their seats to watch my much thinner cadet colleagues as they marched by, resplendent in their swallow-tailed herringbone uniforms with cuffs and coat-tails and three rows of gilt bullet buttons. Since I was also too unfit to be on any sports team, they made me "manager" of the crew team, which only meant that I got to clean and care for the crew shells and scrub out the boathouse. I never once got to row in the shell; I doubt I would have even fit in one of them.

I carry within me the residue of many of the strange messages about girls that influenced the young male cadets. The otherness and sexuality of teenage girls was the frequent topic of conversation and ribald humor at the academy. Sadly, there was often a deep misogynistic streak to this humor, and a remarkable degree of misinformation. The campus was almost exclusively a male enclave, and any chance of learning about the sensibilities and realities of the lives of girls was distorted by sexualized exaggeration, boyish silliness, and isolation from girls. Perhaps more pernicious were some of the values that were inculcated into the minds of the "young men" about avoiding anything that smacked of softness or femininity, unless of course the "anything" was a young woman. Encounters with young women were strictly rationed and closely chaperoned, occurring only when neighboring academies for "young ladies" were invited to attend a dance at the military academy. (For some reason, we were never taken to their schools.) That was the occasion of my first date, arranged by the social director of the military academy, who happened to be my mother.

The event was the Midwinter Ball, and when we arrived at the assembly room my mother's hand was evident. The room was beautifully decorated; she and the other faculty wives had clearly committed many hours and much imagination to the effort. The visiting young ladies, who had been duly bused in, now stood in a line, beautifully attired in a dizzying array of lovely gowns: beaded bodices, strapless tops, glittery embellishments, gauzy veils, foil ruching, sequins, open backs, chiffon, silk, pleats, lace, ribbons, and I haven't even mentioned the shoes, makeup, or perfumes. Hair was either elaborately styled or long and simple, and each young woman had been issued a beautiful bouquet (whether by her school or my academy I never did find out).

All of the cadets were formed into our own line on the opposite side of the room. Our full-dress cadet uniforms were itchy and hot, but indisputably dashing, even for a pudgy cadet of my stature. There wasn't a single brass button or shoe of any cadet that hadn't been shined to a brilliant gleam. Each cadet scanned the opposing lineup, hoping to be matched with his first or second choice. The matching was largely arbitrary; only a few upperclassmen actually knew any of the young women and such relationships were respected. For everyone else, one of the military academy's faculty members held up a list that my mother had prepared, and he bellowed out the names of each "couple" for the duration of the ball. Tension ran high, no doubt in both lines, and there were chuckles and quietly murmured rude speculations among the male ranks about who would be so ill-fated as to be matched with one particular young lady. She was morbidly obese, and nothing her gown could do could diminish her stature or erase the forlorn look in her face. The cadets all knew it was my mother who'd made the pairing decisions, and when the name of that heavyset young lady was called out, my name was immediately announced as her date. The cadet at my side discreetly elbowed me and wondered aloud but in a low voice what I'd done to deserve such maternal wrath.

Since my date was much too large and uncomfortable to dance, I escorted her to a table and there we sat for the evening. She was the daughter of a fabulously wealthy confectioner, but it was clear she had no real desire to be at the ball, although her consent had not been sought. Our conversation was halting and uneasy, but the time went by, and I did my best to be cordial. Throughout the evening I felt a certain affinity for this young woman, even if I lacked the words to articulate that feeling or the knowledge to discern what that might mean for me. I also found myself defending her when many other cadets, in the days after the ball, made off-color comments about her. They were unprepared for that response, and tried to turn that around to imply deeper improprieties on my part, which was even more confounding.

While the immature antics of young men infused with abundant testosterone is hardly a stinging critique of the hyper-masculine ethos of that military academy, I had expected perhaps a more honorable and measured example of masculinity from the faculty members. I was often disappointed. The most disturbing memory of such an incident came when I was summoned to the office of the "Officer on Duty" at the academy late on the evening of February 23, 1965. I was only fourteen years old, but the faculty member on duty called me into the wide hallway and informed me, in a flat monotone voice, that my grandfather had passed away. My grandfather, George Strawn Schwenke, had been very dear to me, and when I started to respond with just a few tears I was quickly and sternly reprimanded and told to control my feelings. "Men don't cry. Your life will have many such happenings, and you need to be strong and deal with it." He turned away abruptly, leaving me standing there, fighting without success to hold back my feelings. The deep emptiness and loneliness of that moment remains vivid. Boy tears or girl tears, my grandfather's passing deserved nothing less.

Fortunately, the final three years of my high school were less stressful, as I attended the only public high school in Potsdam. In the very first semester there I lost all fifty pounds I had previously gained, and in my trimmed-down format I renegotiated my way into high school society. Again, however, I wasn't like the other boys, although I did have a few very good male friends. In time I also had many female friends. Beyond that circle of friends I was largely a loner focused on my studies, until my father *encouraged* me to try out for the junior varsity football team. After two weeks of excruciating aches, pains, alarming bruises, and exposure to intensive boy space that deeply unsettled me, I dropped out. I knew I had disappointed him, but I also knew that I had to quit. Just knowing that was, in its own way, an opening for me.

Finding accessible girl space at the high school wasn't easy. In those days, most of the girls wore dresses or skirts, and while my male friends were taking stock of the girls, I was admiring their pretty clothing or their hair. I found a particularly nurturing space within the school's art program, where a very gifted and caring art teacher, Sherwood Smith, mentored me and provided me a path that ultimately took me to art school in my freshman year of college. His art studio was the least gendered space in the school, and it felt a perfect refuge for me whenever time allowed.

Throughout this time, I perceived myself as a sensitive, artistic boy. My parents supported this interpretation, and were patient with me when I began a beautiful china teacup collection at home. There wasn't any pressure to conform to any specific gendered expectations, but I also had the advantage of growing up in the 1960s when gender-bending and long hair were pervasive among teens. Still, one very gendered memory truly stands out.

My two best male friends from high school, Stanley and Pete, did not have access to cars. I did, and so I was often their chauffeur for after-school and weekend adventures. One warm Saturday night they asked me to pick them up, but they wouldn't tell me what the evening's plans included. Once in the Chevrolet Corvair, they directed me to a residential neighborhood, where we parked and set out on foot. In relatively short order we were crouched in the dark in the shrubbery in someone's back yard. We could hear music, lots of feminine laughter and voices, and soon an unrivaled view through the sliding glass doors into the family room of a certain high school girl's home. She was having a slumber party, and she and her friends were all in pajamas, doing what high school girls did at slumber parties in 1969. My two male friends took great delight in their voyeuristic adventure, but I was overcome by a sense that my place was in there with those girls instead of out kneeling out in the yard behind the bushes. Once again, ten years after the first instance, I was among the leaves experiencing the gender chasm. I still lacked the words for it, but the feelings were plain to me. I was in the wrong place, but I was decades away from the realization that I was in the wrong body.

IN SUCH A PLACE AT SUCH A TIME

Seventeen years later I awoke early to the distant but clear and harsh sounds of the new military recruits jogging in formation on a paved road down in the valley below. I listened at the window as they sang their gruff military chant in unison, although since all of the valleys were still shrouded in the deep morning fog the recruits themselves weren't visible. I didn't need to see them; such groups of young men were a common sight in 1986. Their bass voices grew softer as they moved away, the sounds of their roughly shod feet hitting the potholed asphalt getting less distinct.

I was nearing the middle of what would become fourteen years living in Africa, and was staying in the guest room of the official home of US Ambassador Bob Houdek and his wife Mary. Both were consistently gracious and warmly hospitable every time I came to Kampala from my home in Nairobi, Kenya, and I came quite often. Given the plight of war-torn Uganda at that time, there were few hotels safe enough to stay in. My frequent travels from Kenya to neighboring Uganda were due to my profession; I was the architect for the comprehensive rehabilitation of an older house not far from the Houdek's, and my client was the US State Department. Even though their beautifully appointed temporary home wasn't far from the center of the Ugandan capital, Kampala barely functioned as a city. Few vehicles dared to venture out other than some military trucks or rugged four-wheel drive cars with diplomatic license plates. There were no aircraft overhead; I remember that the fading cadence-calls gave way to just the raucous sound of African crows and the background buzzing of insects. There was no rumble or buzz of a city. Hearing gunshots was common, though I heard none that particular morning. I'd come to hear the sound of gunfire as normal.

That morning at the Houdek's home, a tree in the yard below was drooping under the weight of an enormous congregation of large and ungainly marabou storks; in their dowdy feathered formal wear they seemed much more of a "congregation" than a flock. In the early morning light, the beautiful frangipani flowers of bold colors mixed in with a riotous mix of other tropical plants and vibrant green grasses, all melting into the fog below. Even the dirt paths were brightly mottled in the patterning of the *black cotton* (very fertile, expansive clay) soil and the red clay. Hard bright edges were everywhere; only the fog was soft.

I lingered at that window, knowing by then that there wasn't any need to rush. "No hurry in Africa" was a common refrain; Africa only seemed to move quickly when danger approached. In the ambassadorial compound I knew I was in one of the safest places in the entire country, yet I was still too young and inexperienced to know how fragile even that relative security was. Uganda remained in turmoil, although the bloody, five-year Bush War between the National Resistance Army of Yoweri Musevini and the Uganda National Liberation Army of Apollo Milton Obote was finally drawing to a close. Innumerable atrocities had taken place on all sides, especially against the most vulnerable persons, but no one seemed to be counting. So many women had been raped and infected with STDs or HIV/AIDS, so many young boys had been forced to become child soldiers, and so many older civilians who could not run fast enough had been slaughtered. I dread to think what became of LGBTQI Ugandans in those days. The prevailing mindset still dominates: *life in Africa is cheap*. The normalization of that obscenity is among the worst outrages Africa has ever had to endure.

That distant morning remains a very strong memory of a time that now feels remarkably surreal. The atmospherics of the fog in the valleys of the very hilly terrain, the color of the plants, the cacophony of the birds and insects, the vantage point of the ambassador's guest room window— Who was I to be in such a place at such a time? The sense of being in a bubble, playing an elaborate masculine role in an exotic locale in the middle of a war and doing my script with convincing dexterity; it all comes back to me as a pivotal moment of bizarre abnormality posing as an odd sort of normal. The beautiful home, filled with American furniture and a charming Ambassadorial host and hostess, beguiled me. My "character"—the British-trained American architect with a Florida-registered architectural firm based in Kenya—in all its oddity somehow attracted credibility and trust. Embodied as Stephen, I was cofounder and managing director of Landplan Group Africa, and as Stephen I was living the adventure of a lifetime. An astounding adventure indeed, but always perceived through a personal fog, from the remoteness of being in the wrong body. I didn't know that then; that awareness had been pushed down into a very deep place of denial in my life.

Uganda has barely experienced Chloe, even though that country has been a touchstone in my life since my first visit in 1982, and my very dear friend Byaruhanga Rukooko still teaches there at Makerere University, and my equally dear friend Sarah Kihika still works on transitional justice issues in Kampala. I also now have a number of intrepid, resilient, and very endearing Ugandan LGBTQI activists and community members, such as Beyoncé Karungi or Richard Lusimbo, whom I feel drawn to and care deeply about. I "see" them regularly on Facebook, and a few are now among the Ugandan diaspora here in Washington, DC.

Since those long-ago days of my architect's life in East Africa, I've returned many times to Kampala and even lived that Fulbright year there with my then wife and two young children—but only once have I been there as Chloe. That short visit in 2012 was twenty-six years after my stay with the Houdeks, but this time American Ambassador Scott DeLisi and his wife Leija marked my return in the best possible way. I was the guest of honor at a lovely and elegant dinner held at their official residence, the very same building that Bharat and I had designed and been working on all those years ago. It was a magical evening, and while there were many similarities across the years, the differences were astounding. It would be easier to assert the reality of a parallel universe than to make sense of the utterly changed environment of a bustling and noisy city, the relaxed sophistication of those who joined me at that dinner, and the bemused serenity that came with knowing that, had I chosen to do so, I could've walked the mile back to my downtown hotel in safety. The memory of the Bush War of the early 1980s seemed remote, and recollecting the thoughts of that young person in a male body looking out a window in a nearby building seemed almost irretrievable. Almost, but not quite. This time I wasn't there as an architect; instead, I was the senior advisor on democracy, human rights and governance for the Africa Bureau of the US Agency for International Development. It was still a role, but who could have imagined that I would be there as the very first transgender political appointee in American history in any of the federal foreign affairs agencies? Still, as important as that distinction was, the feeling of just being Chloe was what mattered most. This was the self-ish and real thing; there was no comparison.

BUTLER'S WRETCHED SCRIPTS

Comparing the Africa of Stephen—the dashing if self-centered young architect working across war-torn countries and enjoying exotic safaris while oblivious to danger—to the Africa of Chloe is daunting. My few times back in Africa as Chloe have been familiar and yet strange, as I now look out through a woman's eyes and own my feminine sensibilities. I no longer feel any desire to impress, only to soak in the essence of this remarkable continent and its warm and gracious people. Africa has taught me so much about being present as myself in the world. Words can illuminate, but they can also get in the way, and what it means to be embodied differently while back in old and familiar environments and cultures is beyond my powers of description—except to say that there is a profound comfort in being myself, no matter where I am. Pursuing an intellectual analysis of being Chloe in Africa pushes me toward the constrained and inadequate nomenclature of the complicated and unevenly understood transgender phenomenon, which can best be described as evolving. The science that attempts to get a grasp on what being transgender entails remains in its infancy. Traditional, cultural, and often pernicious terminologies compete and confuse, while insulting stereotypes of transgender women (but almost never of transgender men) proliferate with galling durability. Current transgender vocabulary will do little to help me unpack

Africa's role in my life, and what gender had to do with it. I will simply take pleasure in knowing that Africa has received Chloe as herself—as me. Africa isn't changed by that reception, but I have been.

So what is this change? Gender theorist Judith Butler argues that gender emerges through a series of *acts* repeated by a person, which are always subject to further changes. She believes that gender is conceptualized as repetitive social fictions that are created and built over time. In turn these social fictions are embodied as *truth* or *natural* through the performance of what she termed "social scripts."[11] What were my social scripts? Like all persons, transgender or not, I was routinely taught to conform to my assigned (male) gender as normalized in the American society of my time. For decades, and at times with great urgency, I was trained in *manhood* by a process that has its roots in the very origins of human society. Despite complete social immersion in a gender category, I upset everything by insisting that it simply didn't work for me. I could only have made such a self-ish claim if I possessed a vantage point upon which to stand and push back from. That point of leverage for me, and for my transgender sisters and brothers, is our sense of who we are authentically at our cores. It's a strong if inconvenient rebuttal and not one that Butler and others with similar convictions want to address.

The transgender author Julia Serano has made some headway in effectively targeting academics such as Butler, and all those who've taken no notice of the pervasive "core identity" argument shared among so many transgender persons. My own life similarly offers a rebuttal to the claims of Butler, but also to those who argue that our bodies provide the essential, biological, *natural* explanation of what constitutes gender. Despite over five decades of repetitive (and, I would argue, very persuasive) per-

---

11. In her 1990 book *Gender Trouble: Feminism and the Subversion of Identity*, Butler took the position that gender identity is a "performative accomplishment compelled by social sanction and taboo."

formance of a male script—sometimes in exaggerated formats such as my Stephen life as an international adventurer—I completely failed to performatively constitute a sustainable male gender. Even with the potent help of male hormones, male chromosomes, and a demonstrably male physical body, my gender dissonance remained and progressively became more unbearable. Serano's alternative explanation—that each person possesses a subconscious sex that transgender persons come to discern in ways that cisgender persons cannot—resonates entirely with my lived experience.

At least within those more liberal un-Trumped enclaves where such discussions are welcomed, we can debate where gender is located, and what it means to transition gender. In much of the world, however, the gender identity dialogue is not articulated in terms of "performative" versus "natural" terms; instead it's culturally imposed and not subject to revision on any terms. Rigid societal strictures determine that you are the sex and gender that your genitals marked you to be at birth, and any attempt to deal with internal gender dissonance by rejecting your biological sex assignment and redefining your gender identity is perceived by members of such societies as wrong, or even dangerous. In most traditional societies such as the ones that I encountered throughout Africa, gender roles are highly proscribed and define important power relationships, as well as carrying with them deep societal meaning. Challenges to such social gender structures and identities are deemed unacceptable, and transgender persons' appeals for understanding, support, or some modicum of acceptance are generally unsuccessful.

Appeals for understanding may be successful or not, but ultimately the task of any transgender person is to reconcile the gender dissonance within, and to find an authentic way to be present in the world. Or not to—many of us do our best to make the irreconcilable simply go away. In my case, I gradually moved from a roughly workable persona as a sensitive, artistic boy to attempt to become Nietzsche's *Übermensch*, the daring and intrepid adventurer forging a new life in the relative wilds of East Africa, and later South Africa, and even the Gaza Strip. It was a good, lively, even at times glamorous script while it lasted, and it came close to convincing me of my manliness. I pushed it for all it was worth, taking up edgy sports, going on camping expeditions deep into untamed environments, pushing myself to be a leader among men. In Kenya, I boldly started my own firm of architects and planners, and rapidly expanded that firm to operate from branch offices in four African countries. I lost myself in being busy, in being technically proficient, in being "the man," or "*bwana* Stephen." I drank too much scotch, competed ferociously for architectural commissions, travelled on projects to extremely dangerous locales in places such as southern Sudan, war-torn Somalia, Guinea, Ethiopia (while under the dictator Mengistu Haile Mariam), Togo, Ghana, and tiny, hot Djibouti. The male adventurer/risk-taker/intrepid mode persisted even after my initial decade in Africa. My manhood would be tested in travels on the rivers and backcountry of Guyana in South America, and in El Salvador during its civil war. Africa again pulled me back, as I returned to work in South Africa just after the end of apartheid, and as a professor in the all-male philosophy faculty at Uganda's Makerere University. Everyone bought into the manly version of Stephen, and many were quite impressed by it. I had Butler's scripts down pat.

There were times when I got my comeuppance, times when I knew that it was all a sham even if I had no idea what to do about it or what it even meant. I just assumed that all men felt tested in their masculine performance, but in my case there were moments of unsought gender clarity that left me at best bemused, at worst deeply shaken. Once in 1982, when visiting the historic Kenyan coastal town of Lamu, the oldest and best-preserved Swahili settlement in that country, my friends and I stayed in one of the tall buildings made decades ago of coral stone and mangrove timber. The small but very tall building had an inner courtyard, a veranda, and an elaborately carved wooden door, but the only place cool enough to sleep comfortably was the roof terrace. While the sea breeze kept us relatively cool, a nearby stone house with its own roof terrace had a party going on well into the night. The revelers had only one song, or perhaps they only liked one song, and it wasn't traditional Swahili Taarab music. Instead of that distinctive and pleasant mix of Arabic, Indian, and African influences, we were the unwilling beneficiaries of high volume repetitions of the 1978 hit by the Village People, "Macho Man." The irony wasn't lost on me, and the irritation of being assaulted by the unceasing repetition of this mindless song was only overshadowed by my own realization that "macho man" wasn't me, and never would be. I wasn't quite ready to throw masculinity aside completely, but the awareness was making its presence known. The truth wasn't to be denied, even as I hunkered down on that roof terrace in a 700-year-old town on a quaint island off the fabled Kenyan coast.

Perhaps the Chloe within was finding her own way of signaling to me?

GIRL MISSING

Arriving at womanhood without passing through life as a girl is disorienting. For starters, I'm not able to bond easily with my own seventeen-year-old daughter in the common experience of what *girl* means. I watch her interact with her mother Christine in ways that are so different than how she interacts with me, and I attribute this largely to a feeling of being gender-impaired for much of my life. I was never a girl, except in some obscure inner sense, and I therefore had no female friends at a young age with whom to communally experiment with ways to think, dress, play, talk, dream, flirt, and just be a girl. I still don't know how to braid my hair. I now watch young girls at play, and while I enjoy their company and relate to their activities on many levels, it's still inescapable that I was never quite like them. That deep pool of experiences, adventures, friendships, experimentations, and occasional social triumphs and calamities of life as a girl, teen, and then young woman navigating the world through wholly feminine eyes is something about which I can only speculate. I watch my daughter and her friends construct, deconstruct, and endlessly tinker (often tearfully) with numerous relationships among their peers in ways that boys simply don't. I've no delusions that such a girlhood is an easy passage, and many women have told me that they consider me fortunate to have sidestepped it. Still, it's present in my life as a missing piece; it's a void that

I often feel, ponder, and occasionally speculate about. And sometimes, as Shel Silverstein's poignant little children's story *The Missing Piece* makes clear, having a missing piece might even be an odd sort of blessing.

Ruminations about the empty spaces in one's life may also be instructive in some deeply metaphysical way, but they have undoubtedly led me along a path that's often painful and even darkly dangerous. It's a particularly curious pursuit for a woman of a certain age, using all of the feminine insights now available to me, to attempt such a retrospective recreation. Women are not girls. Adults are not teenagers. It is folly to assume that we can ever relocate our psyches into teen space, into girl space, with any authenticity. Yet the fascinating lives of teen girls surround me, creating a vibrant and often emotionally charged theatre of life that is frustratingly inaccessible to me. The layers of meaning that surround participation on the volleyball team, the almost mystical connection that some teen girls such as my daughter are able to forge with horses, dogs, cats, rabbits, even domesticated pet rats, the expressive intensity with which fashion decisions are arrived at—these are features of my daughter's teenage life that fail to resonate with my own experience, but from which I am sure important lessons emerge that help to shape her into a woman of wholeness.

I'm also aware that my current observer status, and my historical absence from the ranks of teen girls, has granted me immunity from many of the anxieties, insecurities, imposed constraints, and pernicious media messages that afflict and inevitably shape the lives of teenage girls in America. The urgent pressure that many girls feel (or are led to impose upon themselves) to adhere to norms that ironically provide them with inadequate space in which to live authentically—to celebrate and be appreciated for their unique qualities and traits—is corrosive. The media's prevailing omnipresent messaging on the role and diminished value and objectification of girls and women cannot help but be internalized at some level, and there comes a point quite early when teen girls have no option but to shrug off the daily outrages of being so pervasively treated as second-class, less than competent, less than capable, or otherwise disqualified from full citizenship and personhood because they are female. The dominant values of the patriarchy remain strong and seem to be seldom questioned within families of growing teen girls, and compromises leading to complacency therefore seem impossible to avoid. When it comes to pervasive gender-based discrimination, girls have no choice but to learn to pick their battles.

On the other side, I have many unique insights from having been, in effect, an unconscious mole deeply embedded in boy space. Unwittingly, I benefitted from much of the freedom and invitation to be exuberant, to explore, to take risks, and to get my clothes dirty. Like other boys, it was more or less assumed that as a teen I was fully competent and capable (or on the verge thereof), and I was nurtured in the indomitable spirit that white, middle-class boys in the America of the 1950s and 1960s usually enjoyed. The world was there for me, and I was expected to go forth accordingly.

Except for my two years at the military academy, girls were everywhere. Naturally they assiduously protected their girl space from any stray boys who lingered too close or seemed too interested. My separation from their socializing, their giggles and chatter, their clothes, and their expressive ways was very real to me. I perceived this separation with a degree of discomfort, but never with real understanding. Every other boy I knew was uninterested in such aspects of their female schoolmates, and approached girls with a natural understanding and an acceptance of their differences that was never clear to me. In retrospect, it seems that I was then adrift in a confusing space between girl and boy, unable to navigate either reality with the unconscious ease that cisgender teens took and take for granted.

The Chloe within found her moments, even if remarkably few, to express herself from her submerged existence within me. In time, the *sensitive and artistic* label became firmly affixed to Stephen, and the world moved on having made a space that seemed adequate for the personality I manifested. There were many uncomfortable edges to that curious space, as when I was encouraged by my parents and peers to engage in competitive sports with manly determination. I was also expected to participate in the male talk—sports, tools, technologies, cars, combat (historical or otherwise), and of course girls as sexual conquests to be had or to boast of after the fact—although I never failed to be taken aback by the ease, intensity, and competitiveness with which the teen boys and men around me placed themselves in such discussions. My summers with fellow teen boys, working on maintenance of the local electric utility's massive hydraulic pipes, dams, towers, generators, spillways, and related infrastructure, placed me into extreme boy space, grappling with big equipment, power tools in abundance, feats of strength and stamina expected on a daily basis, and long expeditions in the utility company's vans into the deep forests. Such journeys into remote rural, and often wooded, locations were filled with teen boy banter peppered with sexualized profanities, while simultaneously being rich in camaraderie and *joie de vivre*. While I was clearly not in their league, the other young men accommodated me with warmth and only a modest degree of condescension as they took on—and wordlessly excluded me from consideration for—more strenuous tasks such as hefting the heavy rotary sanders, or erecting the heavy scaffolding. The foreman of our crew was a regular employee of the utility, and in his own time, a farmer. He was a mountain of a man, immensely strong and fit, yet also quiet and unassuming. He'd leave a day of work on the pipelines to return home to many early evening hours of baling hay on his farm. Given his stature, his masculinity and authority were never questioned. We all admired and respected him, yet my admiration for him was qualitatively different than my male peers'. I saw him as a father and protector figure, and my coworkers saw him more as a coach. This, like so many things in male space, was never discussed among us.

When not cloistered with the guys on the pipeline crew, I found it surprisingly easy to enjoy the friendly company of girls up to the point when girl space was being reclaimed by them. Those boundaries were regularly drawn whenever it came time to share some confidences or sensitive girl talk, and whenever this happened I felt very confused. While I knew that girls protected their safety and their gendered boundaries, and I respected their need to do this, there was always a lingering sense of displacement. Where was I supposed to go? The equivalent boy space seldom appealed to me except in the company of a very few male friends, and I frequently felt that teen boys really didn't want me within their circle either, even if they were not so explicit as the teen girls in their exclusion. No one doubted that I was a boy, and the notion of transgender simply did not exist at that time. Had anyone ever taken the time to really focus on the peripheral question of the exclusion of Stephen (or "Steve," as I was called then) from either girl space or boy space, my misplaced status might have been duly and explicitly remarked upon. Instead, I was tolerated among both groups to varying degrees, and in time I learned from the other boys how best to approach girls in a way that was expected from boys. It's a story that is probably common to many transgender persons; it's how we get by, but it is also the price that we pay. When we seek to form even the most asexual of relationships with girls or women, we struggle to get to a place of acceptance without knowing that such acceptance can only be genuine after we've begun to discover, know, and own our inner and authentic selves. To be present in any relationship means first to be present to self; only by being self-ish can durable relationships be forged.

DREAMING ACCEPTANCE

Much of my gender struggle found expression in my dreams; since my transition my sleep has been comparatively placid. It wasn't always so. In a pre-transition dream I cannot forget, I'm alone. It is early in the morning on a rocky shore. The waves rumble as they rake over the stones, again and again. The constant breeze verges on being cold; the sky is a somber and monotonous gray with no hint of what weather approaches. I scan the vast and empty horizon, feeling terribly small. My humble boat is sturdy, and I know every inch of it, but it's tiny against the vastness. How will I fare when the waves are churned by storms, or the winds forsake my small sail leaving me aimlessly adrift, provisions running low? Still, I knew from the outset that the journey bordered on foolhardy; so very few have even attempted it and fewer still are heard from afterward. Perhaps they found safe harbor and welcoming hands on the other side, yet one thought hung in the air: perhaps not.

The lesson of that dream was inescapable, but it really didn't matter. Getting to the other side—to my authentic gender identity—was no longer optional. In my dream I'd pushed my small craft out into the surf, raised the small sail, and never looked back. There wasn't any reason to look back—this was a one-way journey from a country in which I had no place. It was time to leave, indeed long past time; my delays had caused me much pain. Despite the perils of a long ocean voyage to an unknown destination, the journey had to be undertaken.

Finding acceptance, validation, reciprocity, and a trusting and caring community aren't quests unique to transgender persons. Nearly everyone shares such aspirations at some level, and most accomplish this for better or worse without even pausing to reflect on the process. Being *in community* naturally starts with being yourself—few falter on that basic premise. Being fully at peace with oneself is a deeper challenge; virtue ethicists and pastors in the pulpit will tell us there's always work to be done to grow into integrity, grace, virtue and wisdom. Yet for me, that basic identity premise was unsupportable while I remained on the shores of masculine persona. My journey to become centered in feminine sensibilities and a woman's identity was a voyage of survival; to this day I never make light of how fraught, lonely, and turbulent that crossing was.

Arrival on the other side doesn't occupy a moment in time or space. There's no lighthouse to aim for in search of safety, no firm footing, and no shelter. No immigration woman was there to issue me a new pink passport. For me, arriving wasn't demarcated by the gender-confirming surgery that I had in Montreal—although thanks to the competent and caring expertise of Dr. Brassard that was indeed a prominent and comforting milestone. Arriving as Chloe was and remains an emotional, physical, intellectual, spiritual, even dispassionately bureaucratic set of complex processes with no finite boundaries. It took both some time, and the blessed clarity flowing from the remarkable poetry of my transgender friend Joy Ladin, before I came to comprehend that becoming Chloe first and foremost meant to become fully human. Such "becoming" is a lifelong undertaking; it may be safe to say that becoming a woman is a process for all women. Womanhood is something to grow into and to own intentionally, as is the realization that "being woman" is always changing.

For each transgender person, being on the other side requires so much more than planting our feet firmly on the new shore and simply bidding farewell to our respective boats, thankful for their service but secure in our new citizenship. Once across my unique ocean of gender identity and living my life full-time as Chloe, my "arrival" might be said to be similar to any immigrant's arrival in a new and distant land. First there's an urgent need for safety and some comfort, a transient place to rest, and some time to take stock. My own new land stretched before me with the promise of sunshine and warmer breezes, but also much uncertainty. Like all gender crossers I set forth inland carrying the burden of my gender history, only gradually to learn that this burden would remain mine to carry always. In hoisting that load I find my unique way to strength and sustenance; I know that for me the quest is first about survival, and then about sisterhood, community, and home. Yet even after crossing the deepest part of that ocean—after having stared down into the vast darkness below and within me and truly owning my own feminine identity—the question lingers. Will I ever be received by others in community?

I had left male persona behind, irretrievably. What was I now, and how would I be received? Among transgender persons the concept of "passing" is at best awkward to discuss, and at worst the word expresses an unbecoming surrender of our hard-won authenticity to the often callous knee-jerk judgment of those who police the gender binary. Are we "woman enough" (or "man enough," for my transgender brothers)? We post our "after" photos on social media, eager for the approving flattery of both actual and virtual friends. Even once such feedback is forthcoming, we wonder if they are simply being kind. Most deserving of my respect for their testimony of authenticity are those far braver souls who've found that their own version of authenticity will only be achieved through claiming genderqueer identity; they audaciously reject the binary and place themselves beyond the reach of the judgment of others. The others, however, will not be so easily silenced; they are always quick to judge. Feeling perplexed or challenged by not being able to categorize genderqueer persons within familiar gender binary identities or usual pronouns, their judgment will often not be kind. I too reject the tyranny of the gender binary, yet I find myself comfortably at the feminine end of the continuum and through unearned good fortune I always "pass" under the radar of the self-appointed gender police. Sadly, nearly all people who are not transgender inadvertently have moments of policing gender conformity in one way or other, so the pressure to "pass" is no small thing. Some transgender women and fewer transgender men do not "pass." Their bodies can only be shaped and cajoled so far, yet not far enough to satisfy what society superficially determines is authentically female or male. There are few things more tragic than the plight of one who has crossed the gender divide, survived the journey, and grown to own their authentic gender—only to find nothing awaiting them but rebuke, humiliation, rejection, or worse. Their failure to "pass" is, in truth, a poignant indictment of our societal immaturity and narrowness, and the consequences are sometimes devastating.

"Passing" as a woman is never something that I take for granted, even if it has long since become consistent in my life. I worked hard to "pass," and I will confess that it was not only to satisfy my own expectations. Each step of feminization had its challenges, some more painful and anguished than others, some quite amusing, but there was also a natural flow and flowering to that journey. I read teenage girl magazines to learn basic makeup tips, and scanned YouTube to see what could be done with my hair. I sat in mute curiosity as the doctor at the hair transplant center talked effusively and consolingly about how many other women shared my situation, as he promised to make my small degree of male pattern baldness disappear. His efforts succeeded, at no small expense, but I never quite knew if he was simply being too polite to acknowledge that he knew I was transgender, or whether he really considered me as just another woman in need of some hair in the right places. And then there are always those charged moments of seeing another woman in a public space—on the metro perhaps—and being almost sure, but not quite, that she is transgender. Gay men claim to have "gaydar" to detect their gay brothers, but I would never confront another woman whom I do not know with my suspicion that she is in fact transgender. I let the situation—and her—pass. We need to do at least that much for each other.

"Passing" isn't just for transgender persons; I often reflect on the feelings of the high school girls who are shunned or otherwise demeaned for not being "pretty enough," all the while aware of those other girls whose appearances align well with our media-enforced, but largely arbitrary, standards of beauty and femininity. When those teen beauty queens "pass," they frequently reap the transitory rewards of popularity, attention, and frequently success—it is easy to detect, as when I would watch my daughter's volleyball teammates interact at her high school games. Like "passing," "pretty enough" really is a state of being that has its birth inside each of us, but it takes a very strong girl or woman to shrug off the disdain of popular approbation because she doesn't conform to "pretty enough." For the transgender persons who struggle to "pass" the stakes are much higher still.

While "passing" is an ill-defined threshold, my quest was to find the community that would embrace me without having to determine whether I was "woman enough"—or whether I was woman at all. I was looking for that community, men and women and genderqueer, who would engage with me simply as Chloe. Better still, I sought to gain a place in a community that would accept both me and my omnipresent (if not always apparent) burden of gender history. I found such community, even if only after many painful adjustments on all sides, among my close family and a few friends, and also among my larger Quaker community. Many traditional Quakers have leaned into issues such as same-sex marriage, gun control, human trafficking, immigration injustices, and similar challenges to arrive at positions that are often labeled liberal or progressive. How would they handle the acceptance of a transgender person? Within the last decade, most American Quakers are likely to have become sensitive to the challenges faced by sexual minorities—lesbian, gay, or bisexual persons—and many such persons who do not identify as heterosexual (or exclusively so) have found a spiritual home among the silent Quakers. In recent years, some Quakers have gradually extended their sensitivity to include understanding and caring for transgender and intersex persons too. Yet even with this remarkable history of seeing "that of God" in each and every person, coming face to face with the implications of having a member of their own Quaker Meeting come out as transgender was no small adjustment for many Quakers at my own Meeting, Adelphi Friends, in the Maryland suburbs of Washington, DC.

When a Quaker transitions gender, the whole community in which that Quaker is placed inadvertently has its own process of transition to undergo—often fitfully or incompletely. The most fitting example of the fulfillment of my sought-after embrace by a welcoming and grounded community of women rests with the nearly 200 Quaker women who gather on the last weekend of each cold January at various conference facilities in Maryland. I've been with and among them at this weekend gathering each year beginning in 2013, and can offer no better or more tangible example of the experiential reality of acceptance and embrace that I so hungered for back in that unhappy 2007 appointment with the doubting therapist.

A non-Quaker's mental picture of a Quaker Annual Women's Retreat of Baltimore Yearly Meeting[12] probably conjures up scenes of a rather starchy feminine affair, of demure long-skirted women, each with her hair tucked up in a bun, clustering together to knit and discuss in hushed tones the most recent examples of alleged breaches of good Quaker order among certain wavering or wayward Friends. Being a longtime Friend, my expectations weren't quite so theatrical, and I was certainly more concerned about being vulnerable to the bitter cold than about the possible starchy demeanor of any of these women. Starchiness was not in evidence. In January of 2014, 2015, 2016, and again in 2017 as I complete this book, I recognize that each of these weekends became a world unto itself. Soon after each arrival my mind, body, and spirit was called to being fully present—with a summons that had come in the form of the lilting soft and high tones of women's voices woven together in enthralling chanting. The words of each chant were simple, if not always in English, and very quickly I'd found my voice joining theirs as I was drawn into the marvelous mystery and beauty that only many voices together can weave.

The remainder of each of these past four January weekends carried with it an air of ineffability and the sublime, of the ordinary and the quirky, of compassion and sagacity, and of tears and laughter. Each of us knew that despite the fierce January cold, there would always be a warm fire in the fireplace, hot coffee to sustain engaging (and often unexpected) conversations, and ample simple but excellent food. Each year, a number of these Quaker women trundled in with lovely self-made crafts of pottery, polished stone, home-dyed wool, colored card, and bright-faceted glass beads to sell at honest prices. Each year many also arrived with bundles of used books to freely share and swap.

---

12. A Quaker "Yearly Meeting" is a loose and non-hierarchical affiliation of a number of individual Quaker Meetings in a particular geographic region.

In each retreat that I've attended, the tradition has been to set aside time in the first or second evening to do sacred circle dances, a form of simple but communal dancing mobilized by recorded music from cultures around the world. These dances joined us together in one community of rhythm, feminine sway, rich emotion, and constant slow movement—conjoined yet nimble enough to find a soft touch of connection with a passing dance partner. Some of the tunes have been of Native American or Hawaiian origin, sonorous with captivating percussion, moving, moving, moving. The light is low, with the women's faces a mixture of serenity, delight, and intensity. The dancing ripples with strength, powerful enough for all of us within the dance to hold in our hearts and in our movements such weighty concerns as healing the earth, caring for the poor, nurturing the children, and seeking the truth. There's always been room in the circle for women to join in or take their leave; the dance continued. And as intoxicating as the sounds, movement, and shape of the living circle always were, I was consistently most enchanted by how seamlessly I'd found my place among the clasped hands and swaying bodies, the gentle smiles and occasional soft giggles. Each year, that first night of dancing continued to resonate within me throughout the whole weekend, providing an embracing context.

Yes, this was thoroughly woman space. Even still, throughout each weekend over these past four Januarys, there had been times when it felt both appropriate and natural to speak from a transgender perspective. Much more often, however, I was simply—and blissfully—just a woman named Chloe, invested in an inner light of warmth and acceptance that was owned equally by us all. I could not be among those women without feeling that strength, wisdom, and light in abundance—a community of light. So . . . I had found my "welcoming committee" on the other side; it had wildly exceeded all of my expectations.

One chant, that was always sung over and over, captured it all. It's been repeated—almost as our anthem—in each of those three weekends, and probably for many years before. Without fail it electrifies and ennobles me, enfolding me wholly into the woman's circle that persists as a spiritual sensibility throughout the long months that follow: *we are strong, we are wise, we are filled with Light.*

RENEGOTIATING ROLES

It's far too long ago for me to remember which sidewalk, in which town, my father and I were walking down. I'd guess that I was still a cadet at the military academy in Delafield, Wisconsin, which would put me at around fourteen years old, and we might have been in Milwaukee. He was instructing me on one of the finer points of being a gentleman, and he was an ideal instructor. A retired colonel in the US Marine Corps, there was nothing crude, coarse, or gruff about him. He was a product of the pre-WWII "officer and a gentleman" school of military values and, in his book, being respected as an officer was synonymous with being respected as a gentleman. Colonel Clarence "Ray" Schwenke was exemplary in both regards.

This particular lesson had to do with ladies. Not about "women" of course, he was clearly instructing me in the context of the duties of civility that any gentleman owed any woman of refinement and elevated stature—a lady. His particular advice in this instance was that I should always position myself on the street side of the sidewalk, protecting the lady whom I was accompanying from any possible muddy splash or spray from a passing vehicle. I'm sure that it never occurred to me to ask why I would do such a thing; it was simply assumed that ladies were to be honored by being protected. It was a role, and in its way this lesson was part of a much more complex set of role-based values and expectations.

To a very large extent, we're each known for the roles we play. Ideally, these roles are a natural extension of our personalities, characters, and talents, but we never quite know how much of any given role is authentically us, and how much is conditioned by elaborate social conventions and examples throughout our upbringings. Roles also contain their own messaging; in the sidewalk protector example the message is that women—*ladies*—are delicate creatures who must be protected and sheltered from the dirtier aspects of the world. That can be interpreted as respect, but it can also be seen as somewhat condescending to the woman in question who may see that "being protected" comes with numerous strings attached.

In contrast to my unchaperoned life, my sister Barb—the only (known!) girl in the family—was at the center of a fascinating family struggle. In 1976, in her early high school years, she proposed to our mother that she wear hip-hugger bell-bottom jeans and a midriff top to school. Our mom coincidentally taught at that same high school, and was so profoundly unsettled by this idea that she immediately forbade it. All "young ladies" in those days wore skirts, dresses, well-tailored women's slacks, or *normal* jeans to high school. Only *certain* high school girls were making the radical choice to wear hip-hugger, bell-bottom jeans (even if such jeans were then the rage), and our mom was not at all convinced that these young women represented the ladylike role that she had in mind for Barb. This was the era of awakening feminism in America, as people argued for and against the draft and Equal Rights Amendment (ERA), and the popular media began to feature entertainment in which feminist ideas were prominent—even if often just as the topic of derogatory banter. Still, my brothers and I intervened on Barb's behalf, patiently and politely arguing with our mother against a double standard in terms of attire. After all, we had been free to wear any kind of jeans we wanted throughout our entire schooling, and so why shouldn't our sister? To my mother's credit, she considered this carefully, and relented. Barb soon followed up this minor act of feminist rebellion with another, by choosing the tuba as her musical instrument of choice, and my mom never batted an eye.

The battle for equitable opportunities for women was really in its infancy as I grew, and I was very moved by the forceful and often deeply passionate rhetoric of feminists. My college girlfriend, another Barbara, but better known by her nickname Beeje, was a sharp-witted, sensitive, and intelligent feminist; she and I would discuss these issues by the hour. Before long we were fluent in the feminist thinking of the day. Together we read aloud portions of essays from *Sisterhood Is Powerful: An Anthology of Writings from the Women's Liberation Movement*, and we praised the courage and persistence of those who participated in the national Women's Strike for Equality. The ERA had just passed the Senate, and she and I were both convinced that the individual states would quickly ratify it. I recall the night on the campus of Syracuse University, just after an outdoor Ravi Shankar concert, when she and I stayed up well into the night in conversation with other women in her cooperative housing unit to discuss Mary Daly's book *Beyond God the Father: Toward a Philosophy of Women's Liberation*. I was almost always the only "man" present, but—curiously, in retrospect—no one made an issue of it.

The gender-role consciousness became rather more poignant on two occasions. Beeje and I were visiting my parents and a group of their contemporary friends at a very modest rented summer cabin at a forested lakeside just outside Potsdam, New York. These were "ladies and gentlemen" all of a certain age, many being retired military officers and officers' wives, and Beeje and I were politely invited to share something about our interests and activities at Syracuse University. We needed no more invitation; we both launched into a fairly superficial yet impassioned overview of the feminist principles that most inspired us. A couple of my mother's female friends pushed back quite strenuously, arguing forcefully that the ERA should not be passed, and that the differences between the traditional roles of men and women must be protected. Beeje and I were instantly on full (and probably rather strident) advocacy mode, fiercely championing the cause of women's liberation. The men in the room had remained silently bemused throughout this exchange, and now the women too were quiet. An uncomfortable silence it was too, and my parents made it abundantly clear that we had transgressed the bounds of civility by our outpouring. I wonder to this day what they all had to say about us once we climbed aboard my motorcycle—now a much larger and more emphatically masculine Honda CB 350—and left shortly thereafter.

The second occasion where gender roles were prominent had to do with military conscription—the draft—and took place on the evening of February 2, 1972, two days before my twenty-first birthday. The Vietnam War was raging, and all young American men were required to register. Once a year there was a televised lottery, where each birthday was listed on a slip of paper placed in blue plastic capsules, which in turn found their way into a large glass container. The container was shaken, the capsules were mixed and jumbled, and then they were selected one by one. The common room of Beeje's co-op was filled with young female residents, who shrieked with amusement as each ball was chosen. Women weren't subject to the draft, and it was a source of *What if?* fun to see where they would be placed if they had been born male. There may have been other young men in that room, but I don't recall them; I do remember feeling deeply struck by the tragic injustice of the occasion. This *entertainment* was a potential death sentence for young men of draft age, and at the least a significant moral dilemma of remarkable gravity in our lives. As the plastic balls were pulled out from the container and read aloud one by one, that selection set the order for conscription.

My own draft number, for all males born in 1951, had been drawn two years earlier in a similar process. I had already been designated number ninety-four, at a time when the draft regularly went well above one hundred. Were I to lose my student deferment, I'd be off to Vietnam in no time. I carried that reality with me each day of my college life, and when I experienced these young women finding this process all so amusing I was seething. Weren't these the young feminists with whom Beeje and I joined in supporting the ERA? Would they be laughing so heartily were their lives on the line? Yet what made this more memorable still was the dawning awareness that there was something fundamentally wrong with my role in this larger drama. I sensed a conviction that my poignant separation from the other women in that room was incorrect. Even beyond the very real threat of being scripted into an unjust, unpopular and immoral war, the larger script I'd been issued had me in the wrong part, and in the wrong body. I had no words for that.

Gendered roles again became a prominent aspect of life when my first wife and I moved to Kenya. We arrived in Nairobi in 1979, just as the Kenyan Parliament was debating a bill that would outlaw "wife beating" (as domestic violence was then referred to). She and I assumed that such a bill would sail through to become law, until we read excerpts from some of the speeches made by prominent Kenyan Parliamentarians. These men forcefully proclaimed the inherent right and obligation of every Kenyan husband to beat his wife, to keep her appropriately "disciplined." Several Kenyan women, when asked by reporters to comment on these brazen assertions, muttered words that effectively communicated agreement with this patriarchal stance. Some women even went so far as to say that if their husbands did not beat them from time to time, they would not feel loved.

Melanie and I could barely comprehend how such a discourse could ever have materialized; we clearly understood that this was a very different world indeed.

This distinctly African gender division was to make itself apparent to us again and again. As the *bwana*, I was regularly deferred to on all important matters, and my wife's role was concurrently diminished. She was made to feel frivolous and inferior, despite the fact that we were both professionals. Traditional African women fared far worse. Once, when my parents were visiting us from the United States, we were mired motionless in traffic in the suburbs of Nairobi. A relatively elderly couple of the Kikuyu tribe approached on foot down the road in our direction, the husband in front with his traditional small wooden *rungu* (throwing club) clasped in his hand. His wife followed, nearly bent double under the weight of an extraordinarily large stack of firewood lashed onto her back. Without hesitation, my father opened his door and confronted the husband, demanding to know why he did not assist his wife. The Kikuyu man simply smiled, and said to my father, "But *bwana*, I must fight the lions." There wasn't a ready answer for that, despite the obvious decades-long absence of lions for many, many miles in any direction.

Throughout my time in Africa, as is common with many pre-transition transgender women even in less exotic locales, I was in a state of deep denial. This took the form of being hyper-masculine, pushing myself to the extreme, and trying my best to fulfill that role. I obtained all the appropriate manly accoutrements: a linen safari suit tailored for me on Biashara Street in Nairobi, a teardrop crown–shaped African fedora, some tough leather Bata safari boots, and my tan cotton safari vest with four front cargo pockets, three front zip-close pockets, and two interior security pockets. If masculinity could be measured in the number of pockets one had, I was secure. I even "drove manly"—piloting my rugged Land Cruiser across rivers that were home to crocodiles and over rough tracks or places where there were no tracks at all. On one such exploit, I came to a long and muddy dip in the narrow unpaved road cut into a very steep slope on the flanks of the crater of Mt. Kilimanjaro in Tanzania. Vehicles often slide sidewise in mud, but in this instance such a slide would carry my passengers and me tumbling over the side, to the bottom of the crater hundreds of feet below. Despite the tenaciously sticky mud, I went for it. That night I sang my own praises over the campfire, convincing myself and possibly others that only through my virile excellence at four-wheel driving in low transfer case had I been able to prevail. The reality was that in so boldly proving my manliness, I had put all of their lives in peril.

I also pursued rigorous physical sports like rock climbing and mountaineering, competitive windsurfing, and backpacking across the African wilderness. I rode horses in the game parks, amidst herds of belligerent (and extremely dangerous) Cape buffalo. I explored tropical forests, swamps, highland grasslands, game reserves, and dormant volcanoes. Periodically I climbed aboard venerable DC-10 aircraft at Nairobi's old Wilson Airport to visit far-flung building projects I'd been commissioned to design and oversee the construction of. Often these projects were situated in very insecure and relatively primitive locations in southern Sudan, Somalia, or in Uganda as it emerged from its latest civil unrest. In Nairobi I oversaw the construction of the new American Embassy (and redesigned a significant portion of it), which was to be blown apart years later in a terrorist attack.

These wild, rugged, risky days were well-suited for adventuresome young *mabwana* seeking to prove their manhood. Once I flew over the empty desert highlands of Ethiopia en route to the tiny Horn of Africa country of Djibouti accompanied only by a young Canadian pilot and a cargo of heavy machinery parts. The twin-engine Cessna flew into a severe storm that seemed to span the horizon, violently jolting the plane up and down. In the process, the aircraft sheared a fuel line, and we lost power in one engine. The pilot instructed me to tie a rope to my waist and tether it to the airframe, open the door, and start throwing out the cargo onto the arid, empty high plateau below. With the plane continuing to shake sharply in the updrafts and downdrafts, I did as I was told, given that was the only way we'd be able to stay aloft. Our subsequent landing in Djibouti was met with the full fire brigade and emergency personnel lining the runway. *Move over Indiana Jones.*

That most important proof of traditional manly success, however, has been well established for millennia: men are expected to be good providers. While I was certainly a competent architect, I wasn't a good businessman. In time the architecture and landscape architecture firm that my first wife and I started, Landplan Group, became mired in debt. When two key clients failed to pay their fees, my banker and then the creditors lost patience. In due course, after ten years in Kenya, we were forced to shut down the firm and to lay off the many wonderful and hard-working Kenyan employees who had become like family. The stress of all of this destroyed what was already an intimacy-challenged marriage, and I left Kenya in 1989 on my own, feeling like someone who'd failed in his most important roles: husband and provider. Our subsequent divorce set the seal on that, and I was left to reinvent myself back in the United States, and then again in London.

I'm hardly alone in experiencing a failed business, and I would not presume to gender that experience of my failure to provide for my first wife (we had no children) and our employees. In later employment I applied the lessons of this one business failure to be far more astute and cautious in financial management. Still, having ultimately failed to prosper on the stage of East Africa, my excessively masculine persona took some serious knocks, and I was forced to learn some humility. In subsequent roles I no longer took such risks, expressed such unwavering self-confidence, or assumed that simply toughing it out was a credible solution.

Professional and personal roles are challenging enough, but personal relationships rely on certain expectations of scripts as well. Nowhere is that more evident than in the role of father. I exploited the fact that fatherhood was going through a profound period of reassessment by many Americans, thereby gaining more latitude to be a more engaged dad than my own father had ever enjoyed. While usually deferring to my second wife and the mother of our two children, Christine, in all things that had to do with very young children, I tried very hard to be a big part of their upbringing, and I changed my share of diapers. I often felt the boundaries of what was socially expected from a dad, and knew that on occasion I exceeded them, but usually that could be easily explained as just being a very invested parent. My employers were generally quite traditional in their belief that domestic obligations ("women's work") were a lower priority than satisfying the bottom-line demands of business, but I pushed that boundary as far as I could. This was particularly evident when Ian was an infant in Durban, South Africa, where I served as Managing Director of the planning firm, Siyakhana. As the "boss," I felt no hesitation in standing up to leave in the middle of a meeting or cutting short a telephone conversation if the clock reached five fifteen p.m.; in time everyone knew that I had to get home promptly to give Ian his bath, and calls and meetings came second. They probably attributed that *curious* behavior to the fact that I was an odd foreigner, but for me it felt an appropriate place to draw and defend a line. I'd attract additional curious South African stares when I would take Ian jogging with me, as I pushed his baby jogger through the parks and along the sidewalks of that beautiful city, or when Christine and I would take turns pushing him in his jogger on trails and barely passable terrain as we ran with the local chapter of the Hash House Harriers running group. Radical fatherhood indeed!

Christine and I were hardly rebellious or particularly innovative when it came to gendered parenting roles. She's always delighted in being the mom, and is exceptionally adept at it. I was the "very involved" dad, and for a long while that worked for me. I did the dad things: roughhoused and took the children hiking and camping, worked with my son on his Boy Scout projects, and attended nearly all the parent-teacher conferences together with Christine. Simultaneously, I took on most of the traditional house repairs and maintenance, maintained the cars, and managed much of the banking and financial affairs, but I also found time occasionally to cook, sew, do laundry, and do creative things with the children. The gender roles and expectations were evident, but not terribly constraining.

I was making it work—sort of.

TRANSGENDER LIFE, CHLOE LIFE

Photograph by Mike Morgan

STILL PARENTING

"Chief"—it's a nickname that only I use for my son Ian; I haven't a clue whether he finds it endearing or annoying. Years ago, during his brief time as a Boy Scout, we joined a throng of other eager men and boys in a father-son sleepover on board the US Coast Guard Cutter Taney, then and now permanently moored in Baltimore Harbor. This large and historic ship had seen service at Pearl Harbor and the Pacific in World War II and later off the coast of Vietnam, and he and I explored every square inch of it. Retired sailors volunteered to oversee the boys' activities, and at one point they gathered all the boys together to engage them in a mock fire-fighting drill. Using selection criteria that only they knew, they sought out one boy to be in charge as the honorary Chief Petty Officer. They selected Ian; I beamed with pride! He stepped right into the role, had the "fire" extinguished in no time and the fire hoses promptly back on their spools in shipshape fashion. While he was tasked with no further official duties as Chief, everyone on board greeted him with this title for the remainder of the weekend. And for me, forever after.

Whenever I reflect back on such brief if special times shared in the lives of my son and daughter, I confront a challenge. How does a transgender woman who has fathered two children find a way to peace and wholeness in her new parenting role? My best path to peace is to see my two children continue to grow and flourish, yet I've not found any way to set aside the burden of having fundamentally failed both of them as a father, and the reality that our society has no room (and no name) for a transgender quasi-mom. While it secretly delights me when people refer to me as my children's "mom" (or at least as one of their two moms), I know that I came to that title artificially and by a side door. There's no way in which I can ever really earn it. I also still retain a strong but now unsettling sensibility about the centrality and importance of the fathering role, and the obligation that all fathers ought to do all within their power to honor the trust that their children place in them—that their dad will always be there for them, loving them in the irreplaceable way of fathers.

This dad isn't there for them, at least not as a dad.

I take some small comfort in knowing that I did all within my power to own my fathering role, but in the end I had to set it aside and create a new relationship, forged from love, but outside the lexicon of traditional parenting. I'm a loving female parent who really has no socially recognized formal role to occupy. There is no "Trans-Mother's Day" to celebrate, which spares my children from buying Hallmark cards but also means a missed opportunity for an important social tradition for all of us to enjoy. There isn't yet any reservoir of shared cultural icons within that trans-parent role to draw upon, and it's always far easier for my children to let their peers simply default to the inaccurate perception that they have two (divorced) moms from a previous same-sex relationship. If their birth mother and I were both lesbians that would be a sustainable fiction to carry forward, but that isn't our story—even if sometimes it's simply too much trouble to take any step to correct such common misperceptions. There's no avoiding the reality that my children have a biological father who is now a woman, and that absence of a father leaves a yawning gap in their lives that I'm powerless to fill. It's a burden we'll all shoulder, but hopefully not one that we'll allow to define or defeat us.

The memory of first hoisting that burden remains poignant. Without a doubt, coming out to my children about my transgender status was the single hardest thing I've ever done in my life; to this day it still haunts me. Christine supported me throughout the ordeal, even though the loss to her was profound and the insecurity about what lay ahead for us both as parents was nearly unbearable. Still, she lovingly understood the higher obligation of standing together as parents, jointly and wholly committed to the children's wellbeing. To her everlasting credit, she never used the plight of our children to blame me for my "choice"—the tragic legacy of so many couples with children when one parent transitions gender.

Together, she and I did all that we could to prepare for that coming-out moment in 2007, when Ian was twelve and Audrey was but seven. We'd researched and asked advice, discussed this deep into many nights, role-played how we would speak to the kids, and anticipated what their respective responses might be. A trusted counselor had advised us that three messages must be conveyed: that my transgender status was not their fault, that it wasn't contagious (so they weren't going to "catch it"), and that both Christine and I would still always be there for them. The memory of the actual coming-out conversation is far too tender and too private to relate in any detail, except to say that the message was delivered as lovingly as possible, the children both sitting there on our old couch by the large window in what was then our home in University Park, Maryland. Audrey, sitting sweetly with her eyes fixed on me through her adorable, red-framed, oval glasses with the diamond hearts at each corner, was simply too young and lacked the emotional tools to tackle such a message. She defaulted to trusting in our love, and seemed to have persuaded herself on the spot that it would all be okay, somehow.

Audrey's constancy and trust at that tender age was captured in a beautiful letter that she wrote to me soon thereafter when she and her brother had settled on a family name they had invented for me, "Maddy" (a conjugation of Mother and Daddy), which they use to this day. Her words spoke deeply of an empathy that belied her tender years, easily eclipsing her errors in spelling and capitalization:

> *to maddy. Dear mom, I am very proud of your change in becomeing a bautiful Lovely woman. I am glad you are who you realy are inside now that you are a woman. I sense that you are very sad that you could not have been a girl your hole life. Love, Audrey.*

I count her words, misspellings and all, as a treasure beyond price. As she grows into a young woman better able to interrogate this complexity, she will continue to wrestle to make sense of this coming-out and what it means in her life. I've no illusion that it will ever be an entirely painless inquiry, and I now know that I can never be a genuine "mom" to her. Where that leaves me, or her, I do not know.

For my son Ian, who was five years older on that coming-out day, the challenge was then far more immediate. Although mostly composed on that day, he sat stunned and speechless. Only later that evening as I put him to bed, as I always did, came the tears. With his large aquarium softly filling his bedroom with its gurgling and bubbling, just one request came through those tears as he snuggled into the safety of his blanket, his plush toy Mr. Tiger under his arm. It was a simple request, and one that any reasonable and caring parent would have unquestioningly supported: Could I not just wait until he had grown up to adulthood? In what was a remarkable tribute to his compassion, love, and early wisdom, he was able to hear me say "No." I struggled through my own tears to explain that I had probably waited much too long already and that remaining "Dad" in my male embodiment was more than I could sustain. I stated it as an undeniable truth, and he somehow knew that everything depended on his acceptance of that declaration. The larger truth that would define his future in no small way was only beginning to crystallize; his old dad was beginning a long but inevitable farewell due to a terminal condition that no parental intervention could resolve. Parents are supposed to make all unpleasantness go away for their children, yet at some point every child learns the fallacy of that assumption. My son's only compensation would be the replacement of that lost father with a similarly steadfast but now female parent—a second "mom" in a way that society has yet to label, and perhaps never will. As Chloe the quasi-mom, I try my best to carry forward in a different form as much of the history, love, and unwavering parental commitment as I can, as had always characterized our relationship. It's a story still being written in our hearts, and no doubt it will continue to be a fascinating but bumpy one.

LOOKING OVER THE PARAPET

God, if she exists (and I do think she does, in some form), must have a wicked sense of humor. After a lifetime of dating women and two prior marriages to women, it's finally dawned on me that I'm attracted to men. I had blithely assumed that once my transition was substantially completed (it's never entirely over) that I'd naturally still be attracted to women, and I harbored a hope that there'd be a lesbian or bisexual woman somewhere out there who was just waiting to discover that I was her soul mate. Yet as a transgender woman I'm now clear that I am probably well along the heterosexual end of the sexual orientation continuum. Perhaps it is only a byproduct of the new hormonal chemistry that I now comfortably exalt in, but there is more than a hint of suspicion that God is setting me up—i.e., this is God's invitation to confound me still further by sending a remarkably irresistible woman my way some day. We'll see.

The notion that men—or at least some of them—are attractive crept up on me. In the early stages of my transition there was an unselfconscious distancing from my former male persona; slipping away from the fraternity of men was an outcome of owning my Chloe self. As I came to inhabit the body and persona of Chloe, I moved from having Chloe deeply submerged in my psyche to having Chloe be at the center of my consciousness. The Stephen persona simply dissipated, with no conscious effort. I've no recollection of ever trying to be less *male*, other than wondering if my continuing fascination with motorcycles and classic cars was potentially corrosive to my blossoming feminine identity. I'm still working on that one.

However, as time passed, one . . . and then more . . . and then all men just looked different—*other*. It was an unexpected surprise, and a revelation that I found comforting as well as deeply curious. Men certainly weren't attractive to me at that delicate early stage of my own transition, but the mystery of their otherness started finally to make sense in a way that it never had while I'd been an infiltrator in their ranks. Certainly the sense of comfort that I'd attained in being *just Chloe* was influential, and finding my presence to be progressively more rooted in feminine existence begged the question: *Who are those guys?* And "guys" definitely in the gendered sense—men suddenly seemed very strange and inscrutable.

The day finally came when one of "them" held the door open for me. I should've anticipated that would happen, but I hadn't. It was all over in an instant, smoothly polite and courteous, and then he was on his way. I took appropriate advantage of the open door, but once on the other side I had to stop, breathe deeply a few times, and take stock. What had just happened? What did it mean? And why was it so, well, pleasant? Having walked through that opened door, it was indeed time for some reevaluation. I was perfectly able to open my own doors, but as Stephen I'd performed the same ritual innumerable times without any conscious condescension toward any of the female beneficiaries of my gesture. In fact, it had been comforting in some way to have held doors open for women; my father would've been proud that this was such a natural civility for me. But now as the beneficiary of a man's similar polite gesture, I was perplexed. What exactly had changed?

As time went by, what had changed in my relationship to men became more understandable to the extent that my perception of masculinity "from the outside" became more natural. While I've yet to attain a natural deftness of body language and verbal repartee that would be recognizable as easy flirtation with men, I at least find men—even attractive ones—very easy to talk with. As for closer relationships with men, that remains aspirational at this stage despite a number of dates spawned from some early flawed adventures using online dating sites. Most men my age appear utterly incapable—or at least entirely disinclined—to accept any woman with a history like mine as a "woman of interest" to them, no matter how feminine or alluring. It's a very dour discovery, but it seems consistent across the sample.

Sexuality was far more conceptual than tangible in the early days of my transition, although the gender-confirming surgery and the undeniably female body that it left me happily ensconced in was an open invitation for me to consider what intimacy and sex now might feel like from an authentic, wholly womanly body. And what a body; even at sixty-six I continue to be fascinated, gratified, and still intrigued by being physically Chloe. There's a certain pervasive and absorbing harmony to my curves, to my soft and sensitive skin, to my longer hair, and to all my body parts which fortunately all function as well as any post-menopausal woman's. Being embodied as Chloe has opened the door to a profound integrity of health, contentment, and peace between mind, body, and spirit. I tried once to describe it to a friend, but the best I could do was to say that it felt just like walking down a crowded sidewalk in a pretty but simple sundress and a wide-brimmed hat on a hot summer day—and just *being*. That sense of owning my feminine presence in a public space had never before been possible, or even understandable, in the Stephen body. It remains a very significant journey to move from feeling at ease and confident in one's body—with "body" in this context being the whole package of physical, spiritual, intellectual, emotional—to even the contemplation of a tactile, emotional, sensual, physical connection with one of those other bodies out there. Yet once I had arrived—embodied and at ease—I've lifted my eyes and looked around.

The world does now look different in important ways. The awareness of vulnerability is visceral; men assume a certain invincibility of strength and power almost as second nature. I shed my suit of male armor long ago down the transition path, and while not feeling quite naked, the sense of being physically softer, more sensitive, and vulnerable to the world is clearly a mixed blessing. Even my skin is different—far softer and much more sensitive—and while I remain very physically fit and able, walking alone on a dark street is an entirely different experience. But then, so too is being softly and caringly touched by another person.

The polite kiss—the peck on the cheek—took on a very different feel as the estrogen and the more than 300 hours of painful and expensive electrolysis transformed my own face into feminine softness and sensitivity. Not only did the physical feel of a woman's or child's soft face touching mine feel wholly new and tender, but feeling the sandpaper roughness of a man's face brought me back quickly to nearly lost sensory memories of those hugs that my father or other adult male relatives had given me as a child. Rough, scratchy, but not unpleasant, such tactile experiences surprised me and challenged me again to reconsider what men meant to me. It's a work in progress.

Women do remain very attractive to me; as with nearly all women, I also adore watching members of my sex being themselves. I'll leave it to the therapists to decide whether all my prior attraction to women was more about seeing myself in them, instead of desiring them as mates, but now I'm liberated to see women truly as fully autonomous persons and not as potential (if largely symbolic) proxies of my own entrapped self. Women as full persons, at home in their femininity to lesser and greater extents, fascinate and delight me; I'm drawn to women as friends, sisters, or at least sister-travelers on a very special journey. To a very large extent I always have been, but as Chloe those possibilities for friendship, solidarity, sisterhood, community, and connection seem exponentially expanded. I count that new reality as among the very best gifts of my transition; being in and a part of woman space is ennobling, enriching, often amusing, teasingly conspiratorial, even sometimes petty and irritating. But it's now *my* space—the first time in my life where a gendered space is truly mine. The best woman space for me are those spaces where femininity and womanhood simply happen; there's no judgment and no evaluation.

Being sexually attracted to women remains an open question. The chemistry is inconsequential, at best. Arguably that attraction is not gone, and perhaps it is ignitable yet, but if so then it's not obvious. As time goes by this trend has strengthened, although I've only attempted to date a few women, and even with them only tentatively. Instead, I invested far too many hours perusing various Internet dating sites, joining the throngs of women who seek out (and compete for) Mr. Right. The old adage about all the good ones being already taken certainly seemed to be validated; most profiles did little to inspire further contact. So many of the guys on these dating sites were clearly pretending to be "modern" and "sensitive"—so many profiles stressed how much they love to cook and how good they are at attending to domestic chores—yet it only took me a week or so of reading profiles to truly appreciate how picky I was. The visuals were important; some of these men (and I was only scanning gentlemen in my general age range) were remarkably handsome. Most weren't. Some were quite witty, intelligent, and expansive in their interests, but not many. Adding being well-educated, having children, being politically liberal, being reasonably physically fit and healthy, being a nonsmoker, and being grounded in some faith tradition onto the list of almost nonnegotiable search parameters left me with slim pickin's.

As for what they thought of me, it was soon clear that I wasn't exactly a catch. In fact, when I originally noted at the bottom of my profile that I was transgender, I might as well have stated that I had a mild but highly infectious case of bubonic plague. Not a single man reached out except for one—a cute, intelligent, and witty man too. But on the morning we had agreed to meet for the first time—for the ritualized coffee encounter—he finally read *all* of my profile. He urgently emailed me, expressing his horror and outrage that I would even have the audacity to present myself on a dating website. Obviously the coffee encounter never happened, but the reference to being transgender came off my profile that day. Too much honesty too fast in the face of such pervasively bad stereotypes of transgender women was neither sensible nor strategic.

Dates did happen; an unrushed chat over a glass of wine, or a meeting for coffee. Most led nowhere, although these encounters were never unduly awkward or uncomfortable. Not one of the various gentlemen ever gave clear indications of having deduced my gender history; while I did not lie about my past, I was adroit in moving the conversation to a more comfortable place. Still, by a third date it was time to disclose. Even in the instances where the chemistry had felt mutually reinforcing, where the conversations had been entertaining and provocative and where "fun" seemed an appropriate adjective, everything came to a screeching stop upon that disclosure. There's no easy way to say that I was once embodied as a man. Clearly, there seem to be few easy ways for men to hear that information either. In some cases, the reaction was suddenly defensive, even outraged: How could I have led him astray so callously? In a couple of instances, the response was hostile and offensive, even frightening. In all cases, without exception, my disclosure was the abrupt end of the nascent relationship; I never heard back from a single one of them. For now, I've simply stopped trying to date online. Perhaps a suitable man will get to know me through a shared activity, through a friendship, through an introduction—although that remains questionable. I have growing doubts that there exist many men of my generation who are able to accept me as a woman. Fortunately, my womanhood isn't going to be defined by their acceptance of the same. I am what I am, and I am Chloe, a woman.

One of my female friends tried her best to explain her theory of men's negative reaction to discovering that I am transgender. "They're probably just put off at the prospect of all those scars around your private places," she said. The innocence and confidence of her statement was disarming; she seemed equally disarmed and confused when I explained to her that *there are no scars*—at least not in any physical sense. My body is that of a woman; no obvious defects other than those that come with any woman's aging. Does everyone think of me as scarred or somehow physically defective? What a dreadful thought.

Fortunately, for some of my younger transgender women friends, the universal rejection problem seems less burdensome or threatening as they date men of their more tender age. I celebrate the fact that transgender women and transgender men in their twenties, thirties, and a few in their forties seem able to find intimate partners and build caring relationships. The problem also may be more about men. For the majority of lesbian-identified transgender women whom I know—many of my generation—their love lives appear to be significantly easier to navigate as they find their way to female lovers.

For me, for now, I remain single and accommodating of that fact, if not exactly happy about the status quo. Yes, I'm discouraged that the prospects are so bleak for achieving my very first actual intimate, loving relationship with another person in which I am truly present as myself. Still, who knows? Bigger surprises have occurred in my life.

REASONABLE EXPECTATIONS

Some of those past big surprises have been anything but pleasant. There's nothing like enduring an unexpected bout of long-term underemployment at the peak of one's career to stimulate a very anxious stock-taking. Where have I found real joy in my life, family, and work? What roles and pursuits really feel like they have a deeper meaning? What positive impact can I really have on my world, on my children, and on own future? How much should I cling to defining my worth through the job that I held—a proclivity perhaps more associated with a masculine world view?

The freedoms, opportunities, status, and responsibilities of a career have been important to me, and that seems to have been more and more the case as I navigated my way over the years to employment more closely aligned with my authentic sense of identity. The last job I held, as vice president for global programs at a long-established and well-known human rights organization, had many of the elements that brought joy into my life. I was regularly in contact with inspirational human rights activists from developing countries (mostly from countries with very repressive governments) who regularly took extraordinary risks to stand up for human dignity, freedom, and worth. Just being around them was a privilege. Through my job affiliation I also had ample opportunities to "speak truth to power" in the various governance institutions in Washington, DC, although I'll admit that

I seldom had the sense that any of my impassioned advocacy actually led to any measurable changes. Often I felt that I was speaking a foreign language, a language about universal human dignity, love, compassion, inclusion, care, equity, harmony, justice, and solidarity in a world that only spoke the language of power, economic growth for growth's sake, political gamesmanship and winner-take-all, strategic self-interest, and often crass exploitation of people.

Human rights defenders and social inclusion activists exist in a separate world that is oddly set apart from international development practitioners, but in short order my employment at that organization had felt like an excellent environment in which to join with others to move a values-based human dignity agenda forward. Still, where I saw human rights, social inclusion, and human dignity as deeply moral domains, many of my colleagues at that organization—along with many donors and funders—still view human rights almost entirely in terms of political maneuvering, affected through enforcing legal compliance with human rights laws. So often they tend to view human rights as a vast global political struggle between empowered, avaricious, and malicious elites, and a beleaguered and virtuous citizenry represented heroically by resilient and self-sacrificing civil society champions. There is more than a grain of truth in these views, but it quickly devolves into a cynical political science discussion of incentives and disincentives, of the fundamental rot at the heart of greed-driven human nature, and of "us" and "them." The articulate language of "development as freedom," championed by Amartya Sen, David A. Crocker, Martha Nussbaum and others, struggles to find any traction among the human rights "industry" or the narrow political paradigms of laws and treaties, which is more than unfortunate.

In my human rights advocacy role at that organization, I still found that the issues associated with the humanity (or human dignity) of marginalized people were the most compelling. Being in two prominent clas-sifications of "marginalized," this probably makes perfect sense. Women throughout time have been so systemically disadvantaged that most of us take this subjugated status and structural violence for granted, and it takes a travesty like Afghanistan to make us cry out in outraged protest at the most extreme or most violent excesses. Given my misgendered up-bringing, I wasn't conditioned to be so complacently accepting. Yet de-spite my assertive nature, I have now acquired a particularly thin skin that is acutely vulnerable to the continuing and pervasive misogyny and entrenched discrimination against women, so much on full display in the past presidential election. Almost equally upsetting to me is how women have, by and large, come to some degree of peace and acceptance with "the way things are," which is really just a recognition that most wom-en know that they need to choose their battles carefully. That being said, the fact that the majority of white American women who voted cast their votes for Donald Trump is simply beyond my comprehension.

Choosing one's battles is an acquired skill, and I admit that I have yet to acquire that kernel of wisdom. In the interim, I bristle when I see frequent examples of sexist behavior—much of it ingrained and uncon-scious—in the behavior of people who really are otherwise good people. In particular, I struggle to understand the men in strongly patriarchal countries where women are comprehensively subjugated, objectified, re-pressed, abused, and disrespected. These men's lives—like men's lives everywhere—are deeply intertwined with the lives of women who are their grandmothers, mothers, neighbors, friends, wives, daughters, sis-ters, nieces, or employees, yet somehow they are routinely able to view women as less than fully human. This is self-destructive to their own wholeness and integrity and to the health and cohesiveness of their re-spective societies. I am not arguing that women should be valued and respected because of the roles that they play in men's lives—women are deserving of respect simply by being human. Yet I am confounded that men have such a terrible historical record of demonstrating genuine respect for the dignity and worth of women and girls. Sadly, and frequently tragically, the patriarchy remains dominant (and often very destructively so) throughout the world—but we've largely stopped noticing or expecting that situation to change for the better any time soon.

My transgression of gender boundaries also qualifies me for that other category of marginalization. As demonstrated all too well by the relatively recent coming out of transgender celebrity Caitlyn Jenner, societies—even relatively sophisticated ones like ours—may be fascinated in a voyeuristic sense by people who make that journey, but they generally don't look kindly on us as individuals. Many people within my circles are very supportive and understanding of my transgender status, but many others outside of such liberal and Quakerly circles are not. The intensity and self-righteousness of the angry, viciously graphic, and highly sexualized misogynistic abuse that has largely characterized the hate mail that my propensity for blogging has occasionally elicited speaks to a certain population who aren't likely ever to tolerate the existence of transgender persons. The authors of these hateful messages are real, they are a threat, and they aren't going away. They also are not open to any sort of civil discourse; they prefer to remain steeped in their venom. Internet trolls aside, even among the general public attitudes on transgender issues and persons are shaped by extremely negative stereotypes and possibly by a dark inner closet of unresolved personal issues regarding gender and sexuality. Until those dark places see the sunshine of open and reflective thinking, compassion, and contemplation, the resulting widespread transphobia is sure to remain deeply damaging or even acutely dangerous for transgender persons.

When confronted directly and in person, stereotypes are relatively easy to bust. In my spiritual leading as a Quaker I have traveled to various Quaker Meetings and Quaker schools at their invitation to discuss what it means for them to become a welcoming and affirming faith community for transgender persons. In each instance, the issue of stereotypes is quickly confronted and cast aside; we then get down to some really important, gritty, and meaningful conversations about gender itself. Everyone has a gender, yet few have given it much thought as an integral part of their identity until I show up and provoke them a little. Quakers aren't exactly a *tough crowd*, but even among Quakers this particular conversation can be daunting.

I have to live in the larger world, and my path has taken me to that world as an openly transgender woman. That genie cannot be put back into the bottle, but as the public (the American public anyway) gradually gets their fill of reading about far better known transgender persons there may come to be increasing space for me to move ahead as "just Chloe." The public adores celebrities; the buzz about the likes of Caitlyn Jenner, Laverne Cox, Janet Mock, Chaz Bono, Lana Wachowski, Ian Harvie, or even Chelsea Manning serves a purpose in diverting attention away from the likes of me. Still, I remain a relatively subdued yet committed advocate for basic human dignity—no matter how I am packaged.

I also have to live in my own private, family world. In that world, there remains reconciliation to be achieved and wounds to be healed before even close family members are truly able to find room in their hearts for me as I am—although I am very heartened by recent progress and the warm embrace of my siblings. After many years I've been able to make the change from brother to sister without too much residual controversy, but tenderly renegotiating my identity and my relationships as a former husband and former dad is the work of my remaining years.

BEING CHLOE, BEING HUMAN

Then a young transwoman—I think she'd been on hormones for a year—weighed in. "It's going to hurt more than you can imagine," she wrote, "but you will have real feelings. You'll walk outside and feel the sun and the rain on your face. You may go through hell, but it will be worth it." Though I had never thought about transition this concretely—to me it still seemed like the magical fantasies of transformation I had lived on for years—her words had a shockingly familiar quality. This was the voice that had called to me all my life. No more distance, no more numbness, the voice would whisper. You too can be human. Now I knew that the voice had been right. I did have real feelings. I felt pain, loneliness, terror, hope, exhilaration, triumph. I might not be a woman, but I had become human.

—Joy Ladin

In my work as a feminist, a human rights and social inclusion activist, policy expert, educator, and ethicist, I seem to be advocating for universal human dignity all the time. People regard this as a virtuous, even noble, undertaking, and they frequently wish me well. Still, it's an odd banner to carry; no one seems to have an iron-clad definition for dignity even if everyone has a pretty good general idea what it means. For most, the discussion is a parlor room nicety, only occasionally verging on a provocative conversation. I've even heard it referred to as the "dignitarian discourse." If such a discourse truly exists it is largely an unfocused discourse, with no clear goal except to make people pause for a minute and take stock.

That stocktaking generally concludes with a something-ought-to-be-done sentiment expressed in varying degrees of fervor or outrage, but human dignity is always quick to be hushed into irrelevant silence when strategic national self-interest or other more pragmatic and immediate concerns are raised. And raised they are, as those whose weary worldliness and cynical air of authority reassert ownership of the discussion, which world-weary and cynical folk are prone to do. Whole books and seminars with that hard and incisive edge of cynicism are regularly offered on topics of the day, which almost all lead to one overriding conclusion: humanity as a moral concept is largely a failed experiment. It is now largely taken as self-evident truth that humans operate only from incentives and disincentives (which of course can and will be manipulated by the powerful), and that violence, inhumanity, exploitation, lust for power, greed, and impunity are simply the way things are in the world. If you propose a countervailing view that argues on behalf of a gradual but largely unwavering progression of human civilization, progressively more aligned with some notion of universal human dignity and compassion, you are dismissed as a farsighted (but unworldly) philosopher at best, or at worst a *naïve* Pollyanna unschooled in reality and ignorant to what really matters: power. Or, as our new president proclaims, "America First!" The question of how we ought to respond to the human dignity of those beyond our geographic borders, or on the other side of that new wall, just doesn't matter.

In any event, I continue to join with feminists, human rights and social inclusion activists, development practitioners, educators, and others with a similar set of concerns and hopes to advocate—fiercely—for universal human dignity. Tilting at windmills perhaps, and even if comforted by a conviction that humanity as a species has indeed become more civilized in the past millennium, we are left with the truth that we have a spotty record in making the concept of human dignity an influential concept. If public policy really gave credence to human dignity and allocated resources, participation, laws and regulations, and behavior accordingly, the world would need to change entirely. So much of the world's economy is built on exploitation, on domination and subjugation, on violence at multiple levels, and on *othering* people who don't fit in. Yes, people just like me. So many of our values are shaped by what can be monetized, making the vast majority of the essential social and community caring and nurturing roles of women invisible to economic analysis. None of this bodes well for dignity's debut as the framing paradigm of a new age.

What would it mean to be a dignified human, and what factors would disqualify certain people? When talking generalities, we just don't know. Instead, we need to be talking about someone who is present, who is authentic, accessible, and self-ish. Dignity, like justice, may work well as a general concept for crafting speeches and slogans, but it really only starts to make a difference when you connect with the look-them-in-the-eyes part of human dignity. I am called to offer such stares, again and again, as I make my case for my humanity.

Stereotypes don't have eyes to look into. So many transgender persons have experienced so much pain and exclusion in our lives, and suffer so much doubt and insecurity, that looking into our eyes to find dignity is never going to be easy. Those eyes—eyes just like mine—are seldom where the world looks to find dignity, much less humanity. Many of us think of a dignified person as one who is celebrated, to whom medals and honorary degrees are bestowed, as someone who stands tall (and who, by the way, is generally assumed in the abstract to be male). In my life, however, many of those with the most poignant and compelling narratives of dignity and deep humanity are the ones who are despised, abused, ridiculed, excluded, even violently attacked. My transgender Ugandan friend Beyoncé Karungi is one such woman of dignity, of resilient humanity, and unmistakable femininity. Her story is replete with so much victimization and hardship, yet she is emphatically not a "victim." She is too dignified to be reduced to that status, and her humanity shines out like a beacon to all those who are able to see her as the person she is, who dare to look her in the eyes. She has owned her integrity, her *self*, despite living in one of the most challenging and transgender-toxic cultures in the world. She continually inspires me with her unselfconscious lesson that humanity rests in each person, of any gender, who is wholly present as herself, himself, or hirself. Oddly enough, "humanity" is probably pretty much perceived in the same way that Quakers look for "that of God" in each person. In either interpretation, that quality is what binds us to each other, that empowers us to elevate our ambitions to achieve not only greater justice in the world, but to go for the gold prize: love and caring.

For many transgender people, being present in an authentic way is our only crack at demanding that our dignity be acknowledged and respected. In making that demand we risk a great deal: humiliation, ridicule, exclusion, or violence because we are transgender; misogyny and condescension because we are women; wrong pronouns and off-color humor because we're just not worth the effort of taking seriously. For transgender women everywhere, we work long and very hard to earn the "s" in front of "he."

Those pronouns do matter, as much as I like to pretend that I'm beyond that. It almost never happens anymore to me, but during the earlier stages of my transition it was an almost daily hurdle. Some people see the use of wrong pronouns as a way to show their displeasure or make it clear that they aren't "buying it." After all, it's a very effective put-down, although after a point it makes everyone present feel deeply uncomfortable as it becomes clear that either the transgender person or the person refusing to use the correct pronouns just looks silly. For the transgender person, even that risk of being the one who loses is humiliating and deeply hurtful. Other pronoun abusers are just creatures of habit who fail to take even the most basic measures to correct themselves before or after using a *him*, a *his*, or a *he* when speaking to or about a transgender woman. In general, transgender people forgive them. We've much more important battles to fight than overcoming habitual pronoun miscreants.

In the end, the pronouns, stereotypes and labels won't matter. We will stand or fall on our humanity, and on our dignity. Refusing to accept our assertion of our gender is nothing less than a rejection of that humanity and that dignity, after we've put it all on the line. While we won't bend to letting others define us, we do need to live, work, love, and play in a society of human beings. We are who we say we are, and while it isn't much to ask of others, it is everything to us. I am Chloe. Accept that I am here, female and very human, fierce yet vulnerable, tough yet sensitive, with a heart filled with love and warmth. I am at peace with who I am. I've struggled so hard, for so long, against such outrageous odds, just to be able to write those words.

I'm self-ish. I have to be. Find room in your heart for me, and for transgender people everywhere, and your heart will grow.

It's a pretty good deal.

EPILOGUE

I finally got that job.

It took twenty-six months, and seventy-two applications. I endured several interviews, and far too many instances of getting no response at all to applications that I had labored over mightily, for jobs that I knew fit me extraordinarily well. Yes, I found my way to occasional consulting assignments where I worked hard and received positive feedback, but never received an offer to convert that gig into a full-time position. The little money I had disappeared, my anxiety grew and grew, and there were many bleak, empty moments. There were also few people to turn to, as most people had their own lives and fortunes to tend to. My misfortunes were not their concern. A few dear Quaker friends saw their way to offering me small loans at critical moments, which proved to be instrumental in seeing me through. Still, the lesson is clear: American society has little interest in the plight of older jobseekers, especially if they are transgender. We can bemoan ageism and transphobia, but our complaints about the injustice of this reality are dashed to silence on the awareness that it is our society's reality.

That's the way it is.

Throughout those twenty-six months, I learned that the persistence of underemployment is debilitating, and I struggled every day to find the strength and determination to stand up against the very real possibility that being unemployable because of age and gender history was to become my sad and rather pathetic final chapter—which I knew some would see as that final crash-and-burn culmination to my selfish obsession. Despite having a wealth of technical skills and multicultural aptitude in running complex organizations and optimizing modestly funded programs to strengthen global human rights and development, I had to ask myself again and again whether I should give up. Just crafting each job application became a test of stamina, since I knew that once they had worked the math of my many years of experience to decipher my *advanced* age, and Googled me and uncovered my gender history, all would be revealed. What chance did I have that any prospective employer would be able or willing to see past the transgender and older-woman stereotypes to the actual accomplished, vital, and resilient woman who is Chloe?

Those twenty-six months were the hardest test yet of my resilience, integrity, and spiritual health. Once I started that new, full-time job, I clung to the hope that this would continue as well as it had started, even though I was employed on a one-year, renewable contract. I had received no promises of renewal after that first year, and from the outset there were ominous signs of a financial squeeze among that organization's regular funders. Still, for just a short respite, I gave myself permission to relish the dream of many years of meaningful, rewarding work at a venerable feminist organization as their director of a global program, boldly tackling gender-based violence, human rights abuses, and the urgent need for social inclusion of marginalized people. It felt like a perfect fit.

Hallelujah!

That fairytale ending, however, failed to be sustained, despite all of the public rhetoric about the importance of achieving social inclusion. Few if any philanthropists are backing up the words with grants, even for respected employers such as mine who are working earnestly to make the rhetoric of social inclusion into a measurable reality. My year came and went; the contract was not renewed.

I will now start the job search—the survival search—anew. Having been out there on the pavement just a year ago, with doors closing everywhere, I know what I will be up against. It will be so very hard. I therefore end this book with a plea to all readers everywhere to see the humanity and worth of every person—even a person who is transgender, female, and over sixty. Know that each person carries burdens, and some burdens are remarkably heavy. We only get through this together, and—despite the name of this book—being selfish (without the hyphen) dooms people to dire outcomes.

Look past the age, past the gender, to the *self* that is present and to the wonderful gifts that each person's life offers. Value that, celebrate that, hold that uniqueness up high, so that the words "human dignity" mean something real.

It's what we are here to do.

BIOGRAPHICAL NOTE

Photograph by Carl Cox

Chloe Schwenke is an openly transgender Quaker woman whose life's journey includes living in five countries and working on projects in more than forty, mostly in Africa and the Middle East. As a human rights and peacebuilding activist, an international development practitioner, an academic, one of the first three transgender appointees of the Obama administration, and the parent of two children, she has committed her life to assisting marginalized groups in some of the world's most challenging countries. In 2013, she received the National Center for Transgender Equality's National Public Service Award. She lives in Olney, Maryland.

CPSIA information can be obtained
at www.ICGtesting.com
Printed in the USA
BVOW09s0551250418

514226BV00003B/4/P